Frank Albert Waugh

Landscape Gardening

Treatise on the General Principles Governing Outdoor Art..

Frank Albert Waugh

Landscape Gardening
Treatise on the General Principles Governing Outdoor Art..

ISBN/EAN: 9783337083137

Printed in Europe, USA, Canada, Australia, Japan

Cover: Foto ©Lupo / pixelio.de

More available books at **www.hansebooks.com**

LANDSCAPE GARDENING

TREATISE ON THE GENERAL PRINCIPLES GOVERNING OUTDOOR ART; WITH SUNDRY SUGGESTIONS FOR THEIR APPLICATION IN THE COMMONER PROBLEMS OF GARDENING

By F. A. WAUGH

Professor of Horticulture, University of Vermont and State Agricultural College

ILLUSTRATED

NEW YORK
ORANGE JUDD COMPANY
1903

Copyright 1899
BY
ORANGE JUDD COMPANY

PREFACE.

A thorough study of the principles of good taste in landscape gardening would be of measurable benefit to two classes of persons,—first, to practicing landscape gardeners; and second, to the rest of mankind. Such a study is probably more important for the latter class, partly because they constitute a larger company, and partly because they control the practice of the gardeners more than the gardeners' practice controls the public taste.

There are wonderful opportunities open to most persons in the enjoyment of the beauties of landscape. Many of these opportunities are lost or only half realized, because people do not know how to analyze and understand a landscape. A study of the underlying principles of landscape art ought to give one the ability to analyze a landscape picture, and to see the various elements of beauty in it. It ought also to furnish a proper basis for the criticism of pictorial effects, and at the same time to improve the student's taste in such matters. These things appear to me to be of first importance, so that I have always conducted my classes on the assumption that, while no student is likely to become a landscape gardener, all are bound to see many of the beautiful pictures in Nature's gallery, and these they ought to understand and enjoy.

At the same time, it cannot be disputed that a better appreciation of the fundamental principles which govern in picture-making, outdoors on the lawn, or indoors on the canvas, is what the practical gardener of to-day most needs. As we go about from year to year, studying parks, cemeteries and residence sites in all parts of the country, we find that ninety-nine out of every hundred failures are to be traced to the evident fact that the gardener did not understand the composition as a whole, and not to any lack of his skill in carrying out the details. The average gardener needs no instruction in laying out flower beds, in mowing lawns, nor in caring for shrubbery; but he does need very much a better appreciation of the demands of unity, variety, character, propriety and finish.

F. A. WAUGH.

UNIVERSITY OF VERMONT.

TABLE OF CONTENTS.

PART I.—INTRODUCTORY.

                                                                                        Page

The Art and the Artist,   Chapter I,

PART II.—THE ARTISTIC QUALITIES OF LANDSCAPE COMPOSITION

A. Unity,   Chapter II,   10
    a. The Natural Style,   Chapter III,   15
        i. Naturalness is gained by:
            1. Open lawns.
            2. Curved lines.
            3. Grouped trees.
            4. Use of shrubs.
            5. Union of buildings with grounds.
        ii. Naturalness is lost by:
            1. Straight lines.
            2. Artificial constructions.
            3. Especially by bad fences.
            4. White surfaces.
            5. Badly treated plants.
    b. The Architectural Style,   Chapter IV,   26
    Unity in the architectural style is gained by:
            1. Proper geometrical lines.
            2. Closely shaven lawns.
            3. Trees in rows.
            4. Clipped trees and shrubs; topiary work.
            5. Architectural and statuesque features.
            6. Sharp color contrasts or monotones.
            7. Terraces.
            8. Congruous water pieces.
            9. Flowers in beds or pots.
    c. The Picturesque Style,   Chapter V,   40
    Unity in the picturesque style is gained by:
            1. Odd plant forms.
            2. Uneven surfaces.
            3. Dark color masses.

     4. Broken ground.
     5. Scattering grouping in middle-ground.
B. Variety,   Chapter VI,   44
   a. In surface.
     1. Plane.
     2. Convex.
     3. Concave.
     4. Broken ground.
     5. Sloping ground.
     6. Water.
   b. In form, is gained by:
     1. Curved drives and walks.
     2. Partial concealment of principal objects.
     3. Diversity in design and aspect of artificial features.
     4. Long perspectives.
     5. Diversified sky line.
   c. In materials.
   d. In color.
   e. In texture.
   f. In season.
     1. Spring greens.
     2. June effects.
     3. Midsummer sun and shade.
     4. Autumn colors.
     5. Winter views.
   g. In composition.
     1. Specimens.
     2. Groups.
   h. In position.
     1. Background.
     2. Middle-ground.
     3. Foreground.
     4. Exterior views.
C. Character,   Chapter VII,   62
   Simplicity, Complexity, Dignity, Boldness, etc.
D. Propriety,   (Page 63)
E. Finish,   Chapter VIII,   66
   Finish demands:
     1. Perfect specimens.
     2. Good care.
     3. Cleanliness.
     4. (Objectively) Good atmosphere and light.

PART III.—GENERAL PROBLEMS.

A.	Entrances, Drives and Walks,	Chapter IX,	71
B.	The Planting of Streets and Avenues,	Chapter X,	76
C.	Water and Its Treatment,	Chapter XI,	81
D.	The City or Suburban Lot,	Chapter XII,	88
E.	The Ornamentation of Farm Yards,	Chapter XIII,	93
F.	The Amelioration of School Grounds,	Chapter XIV,	97
G.	Something About Public Parks,	Chapter XV,	99

PART IV.—THE GARDENER'S MATERIALS.

A.	A Select List of Trees,	Chapter XVI,	107
B.	The Best Shrubs,	Chapter XVII,	113
C.	Hardy Perennials,	Chapter XVIII,	123
D.	The Indispensable Annuals	Chapter XIX,	129
E.	A Few Bulbous Plants,	Chapter XX,	136
F.	Climbers,	Chapter XXI,	141

APPENDIX.

Some Books on Landscape Gardening, 145

LIST OF ILLUSTRATIONS.

Fig.		Page
1.	Landscape gardening in a laboring man's back yard,	5
2.	A harmonious effect in sub-tropical gardening,	11
3.	The natural style in park planting,	16
4.	Where shrubs are needed,	18
5.	Where shrubs are added,	19
6.	The French idea of the natural style,	22
7.	The Italian style in Italy,	28
8.	The geometrical style on flat ground,	30
9.	The Italian garden in America,	33
10.	The architectural style, Columbian exposition,	37
11.	William Gilpin's idea of picturesqueness,	41
12.	A picturesque tree,	42
13.	Rustic picturesqueness,	43
14.	A good effect of naturalness,	47
15.	The sky line properly punctuated,	49
16.	Differences of texture in foliage,	52
17.	A winter picture,	56
18.	Background and screen combined,	59
19.	Street entrance,	72
20.	Entrance to a military park,	73
21.	Diverging drives,	74
22.	A well planted street,	78
23.	The effective use of water,	82
24.	The water mirror,	84
25.	Back-yard garden in a city lot,	86
26.	The privacy of the home garden,	90
27.	Suggestion for a farmyard,	95
28.	The ideal park,	102
29.	The American elder,	117
30.	Hardy hydrangea properly planted,	118
31.	Suggestion for border planting,	124
32.	Iceland poppy,	127
33.	Annuals in back-yard garden,	130
34.	Lilium speciosum,	138
35.	Yucca filamentosa,	**140**

PART I.

Introductory.

CHAPTER I.

THE ART AND THE ARTIST.

> "If now we ask when and where we need the Fine Art of Gardening, must not the answer be, whenever and wherever we touch the surface of the ground and the plants it bears with the wish to produce an organized result that shall please the eye? The name we usually apply to it must not mislead us into thinking that this art is needed only for the creation of broad 'landscape' effects. It is needed wherever we do more than grow plants for the money we may save or gain by them. It does not matter whether we have in mind a great park or a small city square, a large estate or a modest dooryard, we must go about our work in an artistic spirit if we want a good result. Two trees and six shrubs, a scrap of lawn and a dozen flowering plants, may form either a beautiful little picture or a huddled disarray of forms and colors."
> Mrs. Van Rensselaer.

Landscape gardening is eminently a fine art. The enumeration of painting, sculpture and architecture as the fine arts is seriously deficient, and yet it has a wide currency. That is a fine art which attempts to create organized beauty—to unite several dissimilar parts in one harmonic whole. In this respect landscape art stands on a level with the other fine arts. In some other respects it even surpasses them.

Landscape gardening is much the best known term in America for the subject which we have now in hand. Landscape art is an equally correct term, but it does not seem to bring so clear a suggestion to most minds. Landscape architecture is much spoken of in France, but it is unsatisfactory in English usage. In former times the simple word "gardening" was in general use in England to designate this art, especially that style of gardening practice known as the natural, or English, method. This would still be the most convenient word if we could dissociate it from the growing of cabbages and parsnips; but that seems impossible with us now.

The chief objections to the term "landscape gardening," are that it is too long and has too large a sound. By its very look and sonorousness it seems to suggest princely and magnificent undertakings of parks, villas and hunting grounds, and to overshoot entirely those small domestic concerns around which the most of our life and interest center. This is the difficulty we would overcome if we could get back our older and plainer word, "gardening." But landscape gardening does, nevertheless, bring itself to the consideration of these lowlier problems; and it is for the sake of such smaller cares that we need most to study its principles. All persons ought to endeavor to understand the methods and aims of landscape art, as they endeavor to master the alphabet of literature. Good taste in gardening will yield its possessor as much pleasure as good taste in architecture, literature or music. And just as one may cultivate good taste in literature without designing to become a *littérateur*, so one may properly educate his taste for landscape gardening with no expectation of becoming a landscape gardener.

Gardening art offers this advantage to its lovers: That they can everywhere enjoy it, and that with comparatively small expense they can patronize it on their own account. The poor washerwoman who has hardly time to look at the statue of George Washington in the city park, and scarce money enough to buy a chromo, is quite able to grow geraniums in her windows and to have a pretty bed of marigolds and phloxes in the yard. The opportunities to cultivate a taste for this sort of landscape art lie all about us, while to only a few comes the freedom of art galleries and exhibitions. How cheap and simple materials may be combined to give an excellent effect is shown in Fig. 1.

FIG. 1. LANDSCAPE GARDENING IN A LABORING MAN'S BACKYARD.
The cheapest and simplest materials are combined to give an excellent effect.

"Landscape gardener," "landscape architect," "landscape artist," "gardener," have their obvious relation to the terms already considered. Whatever he may be called, the practitioner of the art is an artist. He may be a good artist, or a poor one. He would face the same possibility if he were a painter. It seems to the writer that the term "landscape gardener" is much the best one for American use in all connections where simple "gardener" would be of doubtful intention. The affectation of the title "landscape architect" by those professionally engaged in the art seems to be gaining ground, but it is surely unfortunate. In subsequent chapters we will distinguish two great schools of this fine art, and will endeavor to justify the names of "natural style" and "architectural style" for them. If the professional artists of the former school would call themselves landscape gardeners, and those of the latter inclination would assume the title of landscape architects, we should have a consistent and useful terminology. The fact is, however, that some of the Americans who call themselves landscape architects are the warmest partisans of the natural style.

We have already tried to distinguish between the landscape artist and the layman who has a trained and sympathetic understanding of the artist's work. The layman possessed of good artistic taste and a proper horticultural knowledge can doubtless produce many beautiful and satisfactory things in his own yard; and such lay artists are sorely needed. But for real creative work of any magnitude the born and trained artist is required. Genius like that of Raphael, or Turner, is more of a natural endowment than an education. Genius like that of Frederick Law Olmsted is of the same order. In the few following pages the only attempt is for the cultivation of the taste of the layman. There are many things which he ought to understand, and to that end a systematic classification of principles and a somewhat didactic treatment of details may be excused.

The order and relative importance of the several principles may be understood most easily by a study of the analytical outline. It is conceived that unity, variety, character, propriety and finish are the fundamental characteristics of any landscape,—that these qualities are ultimate and coördinate, though by no means equally important. Each work of landscape art is to be tested separately for each of these qualities. The following pages explain in order how these tests are to be variously satisfied.

PART II.

The Artistic Qualities of Landscape Composition.

FIG. 2. A HARMONIOUS EFFECT IN SUB-TROPICAL GARDENING.
Court of Hotel Ponce de Leon, Florida.

CHAPTER II.

UNITY.

> Every yard should be a picture. That is, the area should be set off from every other area, and it should have such a character that the observer catches its entire effect and purpose without stopping to analyze its parts. The yard should be one thing, one area, with every feature contributing its part to one strong and homogeneous effect. *L. H. Bailey.*
>
> Pictorial composition may be defined as the proportionate arranging and unifying of the different features and objects of a picture. . . . There must be an exercise of judgment on the part of the artist as to fitness and position, as to harmony of relation, proportion, color, light; and there must be a skilful uniting of all the parts into one perfect whole. *John C. Van Dyke.*

Unity and coherence are not quite synonymous, yet the ideas are very closely related, and in any extensive composition are practically inseparable. Thus a number of objects of exactly the same sort placed together would undoubtedly secure unity without any effort for coherence; but several dissimilar objects may also be assembled in satisfying unity if, by some obvious relation or natural connection, they readily cohere.

Unity in any landscape composition means that some one idea shall prevail throughout, and that all details shall be subordinate to it. Some particular style of expression must be determined upon and consistently adhered to; and the chosen style must not be varied except within wide limits of space. Every item of the composition, then, must contribute to the perfection of the predominant style, or must be vigorously expurged, no matter what its individual excellence.

Unity is not to be realized unless the entire construction is under control of one mind, and this one directing mind must not only have a perfectly clear and definite conception of what the finished product is to be, but must also be attached to that ideal with such zealous unalterableness that no item, however desirable by itself, shall be admitted if not in strictest harmony with the pervading spirit of the work. Practically this means that a definite plan must be made on paper. The unrecorded ideal, even of the artist whose conceptions are clearest, is sure to change in time; and since it must always require a considerable season to compass any landscape plans, the first keynote is likely to have been lost before the end is reached, and the later additions are apt to be out of harmony with the earlier work. The plan should be drawn with good inks on the most durable paper; and it should be supplemented by written specifications made equally durable. In both plans and specifications too great care cannot be taken, nor too deep a study made of the whole and of each of its parts; for, as has already been pointed out, it is fatal to leave latitude for alteration in case some part proves to have been ill-considered. These plans and specifications, too, cannot descend too deeply into the minutiæ of the composition; for an unsympathetic treatment of the smallest items may mar irreparably the grandest conception. Mistake is common at this point. Many people, even landscape gardeners, seem to think that if the general outlines of the plan are determined by a master artist, the construction and all minor matters may be left to the plantsman, the florist, or the man-of-all-work. Plans and specifications are not too explicit if they locate every lilac bush and spiræa and clump of columbine, and if they demand that the lilac shall be a *Frau Dammann*, the spiræa a *prunifolia*, and the columbine of the variety *Skinneri*.

It is no controversion of this statement to say,—what is the undeniable fact,—that the best considered plans will not always work out with exactness upon the ground. It is indeed true that there are always arising, in the construction, exigencies which require this addition, that omission, or an entire change. It becomes, then, all the more important that, in all things where it is at all possible, a predetermined scheme shall be followed. The ideas of the author, conscientiously worked out in some parts, give a definite suggestion for the concordant treatment of other parts to which his foresight could not have extended. Nor is it a sufficient excuse for changing any detail of a plan that some other item seems at the time to be better than the one originally proposed, even though it be to introduce some new and beautiful plant not known to the artist. Only a few of these changes are required to alter conspicuously the original idea, and possibly to destroy forever the unity of its expression.

Even in the smallest compositions, such as the planting of a town lot or the ornamentation of a cemetery block, a definite and explicit plan should be decided upon at the outset; it should be reduced in full to paper, and should ever after be unswervingly followed.

There are two great styles of landscape gardening,— the natural and the architectural. The former is sometimes called the English style, from the circumstance that it received its first great development at the hands of the English gardeners; and the latter is often known as the Italian style, from having been brought to a high degree of perfection by Italian artists. It is quite possible to conceive of other legitimate styles, and room is accordingly made for a method of treatment not seldom employed, called here the picturesque style. This is neither "natural," in the sense of belonging to the English school, nor in the least architectural. It is not commonly spoken of as a distinct style; yet it seems better to treat it here as such, and to point out that there may be other distinctive styles adopted in special cases, though none has yet become sufficiently prominent to be named and classified.

These several styles are, to a great degree, mutually exclusive. It is not simply that a landscape gardener is likely to be a partisan of one of the great schools,—though that is true,—but the different styles, especially the natural and the architectural, are utterly diverse in their objects and their methods, so that when brought together they produce nothing but discord. Within wide space limits two styles may be used, but it requires a master hand to effect a coherence along the line of junction. Those who remember the Wooded Island and the Court of Honor in the World's Fair grounds at Chicago, have in mind an excellent illustration of this. Even here the English was not mixed with the Italian style; but the two were separated as widely as the room permitted. One has only to imagine the architectonic and sculpturesque features of the Court transferred to the midst of the Island to feel at once what a raging discord would have resulted. In the broadest terms, then, it is correct to prescribe that some one style must be chosen and consistently followed throughout the development of any landscape plan. This is the first step toward securing unity.

CHAPTER III.

THE NATURAL STYLE.

> In the English landscape garden one sees and feels everywhere the spirit of nature, only softened and refined by art. In the French or Italian garden one sees and feels only the effect of art, slightly assisted by nature. — *A. J. Downing.*

The natural style is unquestionably the favorite in England and America, and probably only less so in France and Germany. This means not alone that the landscape gardeners of these countries practice it in preference to other styles, but also that the laity, composed of people who only feel and do not think, have a profound bias toward the natural style. To be sure, these people admire pattern beds in the parks, and they put into their own dooryards the most distastefully unnatural objects conceivable; but this is due to their ignorance of the value of unity and their pure inability to grasp the real motive of a harmonious composition. In general they have a much greater, though unthinking, attachment to noble trees, pretty shrubberies, green lawns and cool shadows, or to a pleasant combination of all these elements.

GAINING NATURALNESS.

A few simple rules will help to gain this naturalness, which is lost oftener by thoughtlessness than by intention. Perhaps it is not strictly correct to say that naturalness is gained. As a matter of fact, when a house is built or a park laid out naturalness is lost to some extent. But by thoughtful work we may subtract greatly from the artificiality of the construction, and in that sense it is true that naturalness is gained.

FIG. 3. THE NATURAL STYLE IN PARK PLANTING.
South street gate, Arnold Arboretum, Massachusetts.

Open lawns are the natural foundation of a natural landscape. They should be as large and as little interrupted as circumstances will allow. Speaking in a very general way, and with room for exceptions, it is good practice to devote all the center and interior of any landscape piece to open lawn. The plantings of trees and shrubs should, in a general way, be confined to the boundaries. Buildings should be located toward one side. And most certainly should the drives and walks never cut through the middle of the grounds if a natural, rural effect is to be preserved. These lawns may be kept clipped, or the grass may be allowed to grow at its own will; but clipped lawns have a distinct suggestion of artificiality, and the clipping should be confined to the vicinity of buildings or other positions where smooth surfaces and straight lines are already in evidence. The unmowed lawn is suitable for larger pieces and for more emphatically natural surroundings. The lawn should cover a comparatively large area. One would not want the furniture in the parlor to take up three-fourths of the room; much less would one want the green carpet of the lawn nearly covered with such furniture as trees and flower beds.

Curved lines are usually natural, but not necessarily so. They may be grotesque and artificial to almost any degree, but it requires an effort to make them so. Straight lines are specifically unnatural. Nature works only in curves. The planets move in curves, the smallest leaflet is bounded by curves, and your sweetheart's face has not the faintest suggestion of a straight line. You will with great difficulty find a straight line in nature. Inasmuch as the grounds on which the landscape gardener works often exist chiefly for some utilitarian purpose, many strictly non-natural features must be introduced, and in many cases the naturalness of the curved line must be abandoned for the usefulness of the straight. This is sometimes true of walks and drives, which are usually the most conspicuous lines on the grounds; yet the general rule must still be adhered to,— that the drives and walks should be curved unless there is some good reason to the contrary.

But it is not enough that the drives should be curved. There are good curves and bad ones, and if a curve is to be used more thought and skill are required to save it from defect than though a straight line had been chosen instead. In an earlier day the imitators of

FIG. 4. WHERE SHRUBS ARE NEEDED.

the English style,—not the legitimate practitioners,—in their enthusiasm for curved lines laid many which were unpleasing to the last degree. The unmethodical, senseless, meandering, serpentine walks which one still sees sometimes are not natural, nor are they artistic in any sense. It is commonly said that every curve in a drive or a walk should have an apparent justification. Thus, if a considerable hill or a group of trees lies within the bend it seems to furnish an adequate excuse for the curve. Objects which are not manifestly of sufficient importance to demand a turn in the drive are palpably artificial and worse than useless. Thus, a flower bed in the curve of a drive fills the wayfarer with nothing but disgust; for he sees that it might just as well have been put somewhere else and his way shortened by straightening out the motiveless digression. For any moderate distance a double curve, passing first to one side and then to the other of a straight line, will be often useful. While it departs least from the straight line, it gives the most constant change of direction. It also presents a

FIG. 5. WHERE SHRUBS ARE ADDED. COMPARE WITH FIG. 4.

greater variety of views. It is essentially the "line of beauty." Yet it would never do to repeat this form of curve unvaryingly. Other combinations must suggest themselves to the designer who has any feeling for outline.

Grouped trees give an appearance of naturalness because, in nature, trees are almost always grouped. At any rate, they are never set in rows! A good, strong **oak** grows up,—a patriarch of the forest. There soon appears, under the shelter of its spreading branches, a younger generation like unto the parent, and so we have a group of oaks. A group of walnuts arises likewise in another place; and even such trees as the willows and poplars, which distribute seeds far and wide, are found growing grouped together where the environments are specially suited to their development. It ought not to be necessary to argue that this is the only natural way of placing trees and shrubs; yet this most obvious of all rules is most commonly disregarded.

Shrubs are seldom used too much, and they are frequently neglected. Without stopping to call attention to the wonderful diversity of riches from which we may select when we wish to employ shrubs, we desire now only to point out that their liberal use is in accord with the natural style which we are seeking to develop. Referring again to nature, we find shrubs distributed all about her woodland, and especially along the borders of her woods. Since at best we seldom have more than a woodland border in our own compositions, its embellishment with shrubs becomes an oft-recurrent problem. A judicious arrangement of shrubbery will often obliterate more of the unpleasant, unnatural and inartistic features of the grounds than any amount of other material or other work. Shrubs may be used in comparative profusion, because they take up but little room. A good view of some things can be obtained over the tops of low shrubs, and they can thus be given positions quite forbidden to trees.

The union of the buildings with the grounds, so that the former seem parts of the latter, is also oftenest effected by the use of shrubs. A building with its smooth surfaces and rectangular lines arising abruptly out of the lawn gives a distinct note of disharmony. The remedy is to break up, and, as far as possible, to **obliterate the line of demarcation.** Shrubs irregularly grouped along the walls and massed in retreating angles help to do this. Their most efficient assistants are the climbers, which may cling to the walls or twine about the porches, becoming almost part and parcel of the building. Shrubs and climbers together, judiciously placed, will often bring into the closest harmony a house and grounds which without them would have been at never-ending war with one another.

LOSING NATURALNESS.

It is not a very logical arrangement of the subject which classifies topics under these two exactly opposite heads,—gaining naturalness and losing naturalness. And yet it has the advantage of convenience. For it is convenient to consider some things as excellencies and some others as faults, some as commissions and some as omissions, some positively and others negatively; and it may not be amiss to mention certain very important matters from both sides.

Thus, of the prominent lines of the ideal landscape we have said that, other things permitting, they should be curved; and yet there is no redundancy in saying here that they should not be straight. The doctrine is of sufficient importance to merit a second mention. In reality it is often disregarded, to the great detriment of gardens, public squares and house grounds. Yet others make a mistake by accepting it too exclusively, and laying curves where there is no room for them and sending the wayfarer a long journey for which he has neither heart nor time. Straight lines must sometimes be used, but the gardener must then content himself that naturalness is lost.

Artificial constructions, in the sense here used, is meant to cover a multitude of whims and fancies which small gardeners—and some of higher rating—are always introducing in their choicest and most conspicuous places. Frequently these are of the most puerile order;

FIG. 6. THE FRENCH IDEA OF THE NATURAL STYLE.
Good tree masses, with an agreeable surface and sky line. Bois de Boulogne, Paris.

sometimes they are very disgusting. As instances come under my own observation, I may mention a lawn vase made of an old stove painted red; a big rat-trap trellis with no honeysuckles to grow on it; a pile of oyster shells supporting a plant tub on the green lawn; and small flower beds edged with inverted beer bottles.

One of the most generally distributed mistakes of this sort is the conventional rockery. There is not space here to explain how to make a good rockery; but the general principle needs most to be emphasized, that nothing will save a rockery from condemnation unless it appears natural to its surroundings. It may be added that the proper surroundings are not easily secured; and that the small, flat front yard of a city lot can never furnish the associations to justify a rockery. When a heap of stones is placed carefully in the middle of the hand's-breadth of clipped lawn it must be evident to the most sightless observer that naturalness is lost.

Another affair much affected in some places is the little trellis placed on the lawn for the exhibition of climbing plants. This gives always a note of discord amidst natural or semi-natural elements, and it is very doubtful if such a trellis could be made agreeable in any method of gardening. Climbers on the porches and walls or on old tree trunks, or clambering wildly over the tops of bushes, give a more efficient expression of naturalness than almost any other material at the command of the horticulturist; and it is perhaps because of this that they break so forcibly upon the rurality of the scene when treated so thoughtlessly.

The summer house, which may also be one of the choicest charms of certain grounds, sometimes appears as a very monster of ugliness. A long chapter might be written here, also, detailing what is good and what bad in the way of summer houses, rustic arbors and shady garden seats, but it answers better our passing purpose to observe that these are points at which naturalness is often lost, and which, therefore, require careful treatment and thoughtful good taste to adapt them quite to the best interests of a whole, natural composition.

Bad fences are worthy of separate mention. And the first thing to be said is that practically all fences are bad, considered merely as items in an art composition on the natural plan. Yet there are wonderful degrees of badness among fences. Good, well kept horticultural hedges of privets, roses, spiræas, diervillas, arbor vitæs, and other plants suitable for the special purposes in view, are at least bearable, and are sometimes distinctly satisfactory. A hedge may be continuous and yet irregular, broadening in one place, bending in another, and further along merging into a larger group of trees and shrubs. In this way it may serve the purposes of a fence without marring the naturalness sought. But what shall we say of the picket and great board fences which embrace so many otherwise decent private and public plots? What shall we say to this frenzy of iron work which stands between us and the grounds we would so gladly admire? Plainly naturalness is lost,— utterly and irrecoverably lost. These fences serve a purpose. They answer to a want keen and urgent in the ordinary home-owner's heart; that is, to the desire for seclusion and privacy and the unmolested and unobserved enjoyment of the owner's home surroundings. This seclusion is worth striving for in the garden plan; but if naturalness is desired, some other expedient ought to be worked out compatible alike with naturalness and seclusiveness. It has sometimes been thought worth while to sink the fences in deep ditches, the banks of which were given special treatment to conceal the whole; but this means will not commend itself to many operators; neither is it adapted to many cases.

Library

White Surfaces.—Pure white is not a color common in nature, and the dazzling reflection from extended white surfaces reveals an artificiality which is glaring in a double sense. Those who, amid the shining buildings of the "White City" at Chicago, suffered from headache from day to day, had demonstrated to them in a very telling way the unnaturalness of white surfaces. This is not meant to condemn the style so freely adopted at the World's Fair. The white buildings certainly gave a striking and in many ways an enjoyable effect. Yet there were some things to be said against them. On a small scale, with buildings of more trivial architecture, white painting is seldom admissible among plantings of a naturalistic accent. Yet note how often we are compelled to look at white houses, especially among farmhouses, where the exclusively and perhaps beautifully rural landscape is least prepared to receive them. It is safe to say that white surfaces and natural effects are always incongruous.

Badly Treated Plants.—There are many unnatural methods of plant training in vogue; and it goes without saying that they are inconsistent with the English style. Yet we constantly find them intermingled with purely natural objects, much to the detriment of both. The junipers, boxes, arbor vitæs and similar plants trimmed into smooth cones, vases, globes and more complex combinations, illustrate this method. Weeping tops grafted on straight, upright trunks belong to the same class. Others might be mentioned, some good and some bad in themselves, but all agreeing in the certainty with which they spoil the unity of any place in which informal treatment is essayed.

CHAPTER IV.

THE ARCHITECTURAL STYLE.

> The evident harmony of arrangement between the house and surrounding landscape is what first strikes one in Italian landscape architecture,—the design as a whole, including gardens, terraces, groves, and their necessary surroundings and embellishments, it being clear that no one of these component parts was ever considered independently, the architect of the house being also the architect of the garden and the rest of the villa. — *Charles A. Platt.*

A number of terms, all equally clear and useful, have been used for this well-defined style of gardening. We need to notice three,—architectural, geometrical and Italian. Of these the first is best for our purposes, especially if architecture is understood in the broadest sense to include all the exterior accessories of buildings, to which the work of the architect may rightfully extend. Columns, obelisks, arches, fountains, statues and groups of statuary, and all similar structures whatsoever, are in this sense included within the common range of architecture and architectural gardening. Indeed, the earliest and some of the best examples of this style which we have were planned and executed by professional architects,—men who did not claim to be gardeners at all. The term "geometrical" has its obvious signification. It is perfectly legitimate, and in many places highly serviceable. This method is also widely and properly known as the Italian style, having received its best development in Italy.

The architectural style is diametrically opposed at all points to the extreme natural style. It is opposite in methods and in effects; though this is no reason why a person of artistic taste may not find full satisfaction in either. The most modern tendency is to admit the architectural, the natural and all other possible styles of gardening, to equal consideration; to recognize that each may claim greatest advantages in special situations; and to choose from among different styles, in a frame of mind quite free from prejudice, the one best suited to any given circumstances of environment and demand. The time was,—and recently,—when English and American gardeners were very much prejudiced against geometrical methods of all sorts. As a result, their attempted naturalistic effects were forced into situations where grievous failure alone could meet them, but where a less partisan good taste would have wrought beautiful and satisfying results through the discredited methods. One of the most renowned specimens of the Italian style is shown in Fig. 7.

Two things especially have contributed in recent years to an honest appreciation in America of the claims of the architectural style. One is the favorable attitude of discriminating praise on the part of almost all American writers, more emphatically presented in Mr. Charles A. Platt's book, "Italian Gardens." The second cause is the satisfaction and delight felt by all in the wonderful architectonic outdoor effects realized at the World's Fair. It is not so much that the gardening architecture of the World's Fair was so much grander in size, extent and artistic conception than anything we had previously had on this continent, as it is that it was seen by so many hundreds of thousands of people from all parts of America, to most of whom this architectural glory came as a revelation.

Before beginning to point out the specific contrivances by which the perfection of the architectural style is sought, it will be best to consider its broader relations, conditions and limitations. The architectural garden is, in a very proper sense, an extension,—a development

FIG. 7. THE ITALIAN STYLE IN ITALY.
Grounds of the Casino at Monte Carlo.

of the building or buildings in contiguity. A dwelling house must have porches, promenades, provision for the exercise, rest or enjoyment of its inhabitants in the open air, with more or less protection under foot and overhead. A public building must have its colonnades, loggias and approaches. These may extend indefinitely away from the proper walls of the building and into the area of the garden. It is necessary only to keep up a close and obvious connection between the entrance steps, the walks of stone or marble flagging, the resting seats of hewn stone, the fountains, the statuary and the stone boundary walls, to see how completely the main edifice may extend quite to the boundary of the grounds.

Looking at it in this light it is manifest that the surrounding grounds, developed from the central building, are accessory and subordinate to it. They serve as an appropriate frame in which to exhibit the beauty of the building. They do not attempt to hide the main work of architecture, nor to draw attention away from it, but to point out and emphasize its beauties. It would be well if this point were borne in mind by landscape gardeners in general; for there are many cases in which the buildings are of supreme interest, and any gardening which openly competes with them for public attention and admiration is pronouncedly intolerable. It is doubtful if any naturalistic effects should ever be attempted in such cases. It can be fairly said that the possibilities of developing such places after the Italian methods are seldom realized in this country; for while we have a great deal of painfully unnatural gardening, we have wofully little creditable architectural adornment outside the paint which covers our houses.

The principle of choice between the two great styles has already been pointed out. In situations where the buildings are necessarily predominant, the architectural style is more easy of application, while in those cases

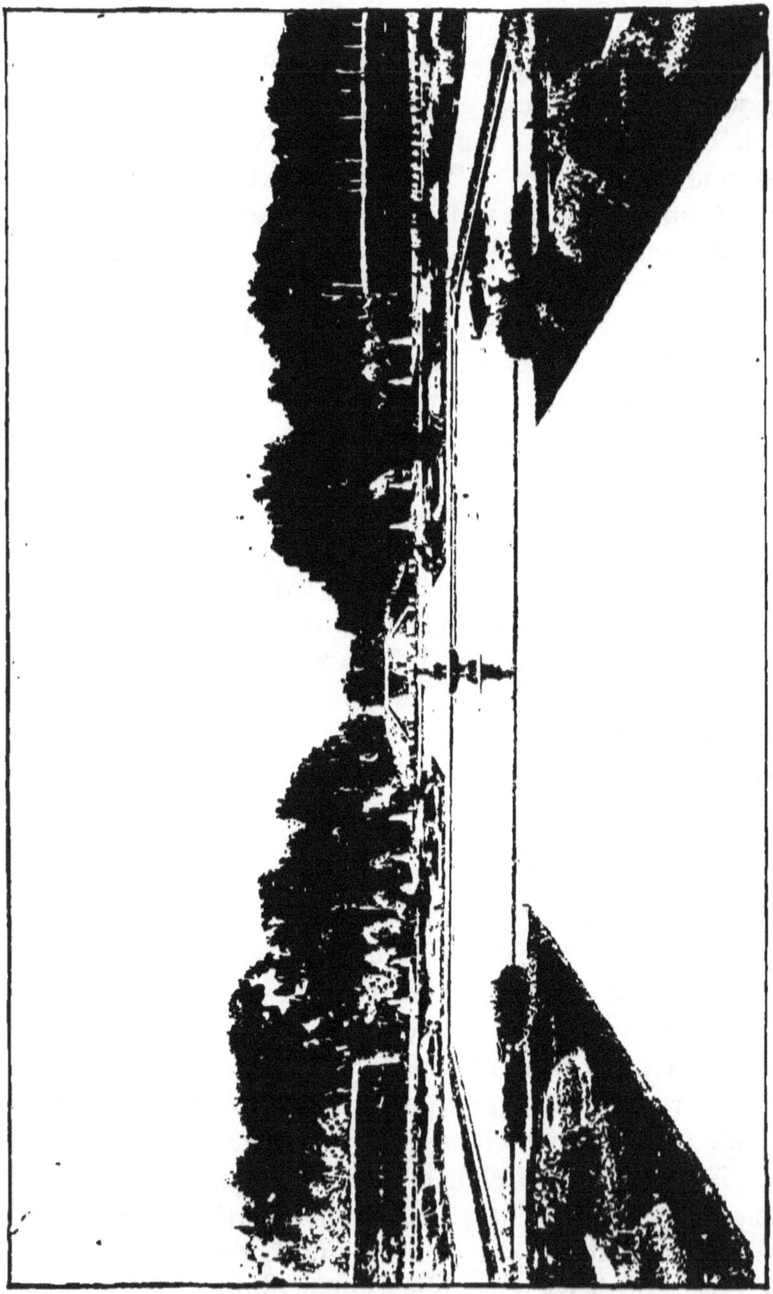

30 LANDSCAPE GARDENING.

FIG. 8. THE GEOMETRICAL STYLE ON FLAT GROUND. FRANCE.

where the grounds are naturally of chief importance, they respond most readily and satisfactorily to the natural style of development. This rule may not be proof against exceptions, but it is safe.

One word more needs to be said. A compromise or combination of the two styles—the natural and the architectural—is utterly irrational and impossible. Certain concessions to architecture are always necessary in natural gardening, even in Yellowstone National Park, but they must always be looked upon as detracting from the ideal, and their thoughtless introduction or unskillful treatment may quickly damage the naturalistic landscape beyond repair. And so must flowers, foliage and trees be brought into the architectural garden, but they must, by heroic efforts, be subordinated to the geometrical outlines of the main features.

Geometrical lines, always to be avoided in naturalistic gardening, are to be conservatively sought in working out the architectural ideal. Flower beds, borders, drives, walks, and all other similar elements of the landscape, which in naturalistic compositions would preferably be expressed in flowing curves, will in this style be set in straight lines and geometrical curves. There are pleasing geometrical lines, and unpleasing ones. More truly are there good combinations of geometrical lines, and bad ones. To discriminate between the good and the bad requires the same taste that is needed to criticise any other art object. To originate a good one in the imagination and successfully to transfer it to the garden, requires the mind and the education of an artist.

The amateur may remember that these three tests can safely be applied to his geometrical tracings: Simplicity, boldness, grace. Simplicity is of supreme importance. Intricate or complex geometrical designs, which do not appear at once clear and reasonable, even at the first careless, inattentive glance, are curiosities fit for intellectual study, and not elements of a picture for the delight of the more subtle æsthetic faculties. They might serve a purpose in a museum. In a garden they have no place. This is especially to be insisted on at this point, for the novice can easily combine geometrical forms; but doing so without training and without sympathy, his work is at best grotesque, and quite apt to be silly. This same lack of feeling for dignity of outline results in tameness, weakness, puerility, in place of that quality which we have designated as boldness. We might have called this quality dignity; but dignity is both simple and bold. Now if simplicity and boldness alone were demanded of geometrical lines, perfection would be within easy reach. One would have only to confine himself to rectangular combinations to achieve both. But some more graceful outlines are desired by the eye, and to their invention the designer may well give earnest study. No definition of grace, in this sense, can be put in words, much less any directions by which its realization may be effectually secured.

The lawn has already been referred to as being in a double sense the ground work of the garden picture. The close shaven lawn is the very life of the architectural garden. Often it is all the garden there is to the composition. If a city residence crowds upon a busy street, trees, shrubs and flowers are all impracticable; but the little strip of close cut grass between is clean, cool and comfortable. A court yard may be chiefly concerned with a fountain, stone flagging and heavy benches; but there may be some little patches of clipped grass in between, and these will be like the carpets within the building. The uncut lawn with grass running riot is so evidently out of unity with all architectonic features as to need no remark.

Trees set in rows may or may not add to the perfection of the Italian style. If trees are to be used in any

THE ARCHITECTURAL STYLE. 33

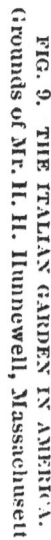

FIG. 9. THE ITALIAN GARDEN IN AMERICA.
Grounds of Mr. H. H. Hunnewell, Massachusetts.

moderate number they should usually stand in **rows**; and if they approach closely to some extended geometrical line they should always be placed parallel to it. This applies to those infrequent instances in which a row of trees will appear next the long face of a building, and to the more common cases in which they will follow a drive or walk. It is quite the delight of the landscape architect to form long avenues of stately trees; and how successful such leafy avenues have been in satisfying the longings of men's hearts one need only consult the historian, the story writer and the poet to learn.

Street planting should be referred, for discussion, to this place in our outline; and it is a matter of such general importance, and yet one in which such a surprising amount of bad taste is displayed, that we may give it a proportionally large amount of our attention. The street, then, is to be regarded as a geometrical figure, and is to be consistently treated as such. This requires three things. First, the rows should be parallel with the street. Second, the trees should be set at uniform distances. Third, the individual trees should be just as nearly uniform in all respects as it is possible to make them. The first two considerations are sufficiently obvious. The third rule is constantly violated. It is not at all uncommon to find two or more distinct species mixed together in the same row. The writer remembers to have seen nine different species in a single row running only half the length of a city block. This row was purposely set in such an order by the enthusiastic owner of the property. The man might consistently have sewed nine monstrously different buttons in a row down the front of his Prince Albert coat. Great effort should further be made to have all the trees in any given row of the same size and form. If in the first planting of a street only a part of the trees grow, no time or pains can be spared quickly to fill the vacancies. And during the early development of the row attention should be given to favor the slow growing specimens and to check the strong. After a row of trees of a single species is well started, a satisfactory uniformity will usually result without further special attention. It is, of course, not desirable to try to make each elm tree along an avenue the exact counterpart of some model;* but with trees of more precise forms even this effort is worth while. There are some species of trees having forms almost architectural in themselves, such as the Lombardy poplar; and for purely ornamental purposes such trees may be used with marked success along avenues. Other trees, as arbor vitæs, which can be clipped into distinctly geometrical forms, might undoubtedly be used with abundant satisfaction in certain cases for the same purposes.

Clipped trees and shrubs are frequently seen in the little gardens about our city and country residences. But among the numerous specimens of this sort which one finds, it is hard indeed to find one which really adds some value to the scene. They are usually mere freaks of the gardeners' imagination. They should be severely discouraged. But in a consistently developed Italian garden, judiciously placed among harmonious surroundings, these clipped plants may become beautiful and dignified. The clipped hedges of the Italian villas are a most delightful part of the compositions. In some of these, sculptured columns are set at regular distances, fitting snugly into the mass of the hedge plants; and thus the architectural effect is accented and improved.

Topiary work was extremely fashionable among the gardeners of England and the continent in the years pre-

---

* Special effort is required, however, to make a good avenue of elms. The diversities of form are often so serious as to detract materially from the beauty of the row. This difficulty may be overcome, when the work is of sufficient importance, by planting well selected grafted trees. See also Chapter X, Part III.

ceding the development of the natural style. It was more used there than in Italy, and without the related features of the Italian style. Topiary work consists in the clipping of trees or shrubs into more elaborate architectural or statuesque forms, such as to make whole arbors, statues, and often ingeniously grotesque figures. If it is useful anywhere it may be brought into the architectural garden; but its extravagances are always unbearable, and are now haply out of vogue.

The introduction of stairways, balustrades, urns, fountains and statues in a much-frequented garden, supposing the articles to be in themselves pleasing, must always be a satisfaction to the human habitues. The eye delights in them all. So that when we have quite laid aside the attempt to deceive the senses into a feeling of rural solitude, and are working along professedly artificial lines, nothing gives greater pleasure than well-executed and well disposed architectural and sculpturesque features. This proposition needs no argument or explanation. It is self-evident, but none the less pregnant for its obviousness.

The colors which seem most in unison with architectural gardening are the deep green monotones in the clipped walls and columns. A mixture of colors in these would spoil forever their dignity and repose. A spotted wall or a variegated column would be an absurdity. But sharp contrasts are in some places also useful, as in the practice of setting white marble statues against walls of the darkest green. For the blossoming plants which are sometimes used in beds or pots, bright and contrasting colors are to be chosen. This practice is also entirely the opposite of that employed in the natural style, where the most delicate gradations of greens and grays are contrived.

A terrace always presents two or three parallel lines, according to its construction. These should be exactly

THE ARCHITECTURAL STYLE. 37

FIG. 10. THE ARCHITECTURAL STYLE. Court of Honor, Columbian Exposition, Chicago. One of the finest examples ever produced.

parallel and geometrical in outline. They are in any case purely formal, geometrical, architectural; and they fit easily into an architectural composition and measurably enhance its effect.

Fountains are always appropriate to the style of gardening here under consideration. But limited stretches of still water, bound in by stone steps, walls or edgings, also serve to beautify the scene while still further heightening the effect which we are now seeking. It may perhaps be permissible to refer again to the Court of Honor at the World's Fair in illustration of the wonderful effectiveness of water surfaces amid architectural surroundings. The free use of water pieces in gardens was a chief tenent of the Moorish, Persian and Indian gardeners, and may be said to be the principal attraction of so much of their work as remains to the present day.

Flower beds were notable features of the old Italian villas. The typical disposition of them was within an enclosure walled by sheared trees, as already described. Within these environs a large number of small flower beds were laid off in geometrical shapes, edged with low clipped borders of grass or shrubs, and separated by graveled walks. Both hardy perennial plants and flowering annuals were used in these little plots. Outside these gardens, in any suitable position, flowering or foliage plants may be found in pots or boxes. These receptacles may be at the successive posts of a horizontal balustrade; they may surmount the newel posts at the foot of some stairs, or they may flank a path-side garden seat. The lawn vases, such as one sees quite too often on naturalistically treated lawns, may be used in this style with greater freedom.

Pattern bedding should be mentioned here because it does not belong to the architectural ideal, though some people may suppose that it does. Indeed, the pattern beds such as we see so distastefully displayed in our parks, showing in gaudy colei and acalyphas the day of the week, a map of the United States or an ugly ship sailing on dry land,—these things do not belong to any system of landscape gardening. Neither do the trivial little mosaics of echeverias and geraniums which one sees in private dooryards. These things belong in the horticultural museum, along with other oddities and monstrosities. It is not possible to speak of gardening as a fine art until these things are thoroughly forsaken and forgotten.

CHAPTER V.

THE PICTURESQUE STYLE.

> But regularity can never attain to a great share of beauty, and to none of the species called picturesque; a denomination in general expressive of excellence, but which, by being too indiscriminately applied, may be sometimes productive of errors. — *Thomas Wheatley.*
>
> Nay, farther, we do not scruple to assert that roughness forms the most essential point of difference between the beautiful and the picturesque. — *William Gilpin.*
>
> L'irrégularité est l'essence du pittoresque. — *Edouard André.*

This chapter is introduced for two purposes: First, to treat of a quality in landscape composition which, if carried out to a considerable extent, produces a style really different from either of those already treated; and, second, to represent any number of additional styles of landscape gardening beyond the two generally recognized. There are no common, well defined and well known styles except the natural and the architectural; but there is no essential reason why there should not be. It may even be regarded as desirable that there shall arise some school of artists with sufficient keenness of invention and purity of feeling to create some really new styles for us. At present it comes best within the range of our study to call attention to the peculiar quality of picturesqueness; and to suggest that it may, in some situations, be emphasized over a considerable space. In such a case the picturesque is essentially a distinct style.

There are many plant forms which are picturesque in themselves, and which may best illustrate the nature of this quality to anyone not clearly understanding what it is. Such forms are those of the gingko tree, Table Mountain pine, Weeping Norway spruce, Weeping larch,

THE PICTURESQUE STYLE. 41

Wier's Cut Leaved maple, the leafless Kentucky coffee tree, and many others. No general definition of picturesqueness, as applied thus to plants, can well be given so as to enable an inexperienced eye to select them from the arboretum. But the landscape gardener, in whose mind the ideal is clearly conceived, will have small difficulty in finding the plants suited to its expression.

A broken and uneven surface is especially adapted to the production of picturesque effects. Indeed, it is not

FIG. 11. WILLIAM GILPIN'S IDEA OF PICTURESQUENESS.
From his "Forest Scenery."

improper, though not strictly correct for all cases, to designate the peculiar beauties of mountain scenery as picturesqueness. Mountain scenery is not commonly architectural in style; neither does it have the smooth and flowing outlines of the English ideal garden. Should a landscape gardener some time find himself with a piece of mountain ground to work upon, he would hardly be excusable should he attempt any other treatment than the picturesque effects usually found in such places.

Dark color masses and monotones have often a weird and picturesque suggestion for the sympathetic mind. This is even the case when expressed in the formal outlines of the architectural style; but it is more

FIG. 12. A PICTURESQUE TREE. TABLE MOUNTAIN PINE.

strikingly true when the dark monotones appear in masses of black spruces, or similarly dark foliaged plants. The deep, dark shadows of mountain sides add noticeably to the effectiveness of the scene, and to the quality here considered.

A much broken sky line is not always desirable in other styles of gardening, particularly in the natural. It is, indeed, one of the first points of instruction usually given in attempts to teach the natural style, that the sky line should be broken; but this expedient for variety may well have its limits in most naturalistic compositions. In a development of the picturesque it has practically no limit, and the more the sky line may be serried and cut the more emphatic will be the resulting effect.

The scattering specimens of starved and deformed pines which one sees at some places on rugged hill or mountain sides have a charming picturesqueness in themselves which fits well into their surroundings. Solid groups of symmetrically developed trees in such

FIG. 13. RUSTIC PICTURESQUENESS.
From a California park.

situations would be patent detractions from the general local effect. The scattering individuals have a great advantage, and these are best displayed in middle distances. A single tree is always a middle-ground subject. If it be too close to the observer its composite beauty is unseen; if it be too far, its individuality is blurred. All this is of especial weight in a specimen exhibited for its individual eccentricities. It has even been the practice in some instances to plant dead and blasted trees in pleasure grounds for the picturesqueness of their effect, but the expediency of such a plan is very questionable.

CHAPTER VI.

VARIETY.

> Nature puts so much variety into her reality that she is more beautiful than we can imagine by sheer force of quantity! Ten days for an artist in a mountain valley will give him ten views from the same point which will be entirely different each day. *F. Schuyler Mathews.*
>
> Gettiamo un rapido sguardo sul vasto imperio delle arti, osserviamo per poco le produzioni di ciascuna, e resteremo convitti che, nulla è bello alla ragione se non le si presenta con parti varie, e queste riunite in un principo comune. *F. Cartolano.*

Thus far we have been treating of unity, and pointing out those particular elements which are usually harmonious when brought together. Unity must always be placed first, as the most important quality; for sometimes unity alone will make a small composition agreeable. Still, if unity means uniformity, sameness, the eye soon tires of it. But unity does not demand sameness. There may be unity with variety. The two are not really opposed to each other, though either one would be easier to accomplish could the other be disregarded. Perfect unity with satisfying variety need not be even a compromise; but both tests must always be applied by the gardener. It is helpful to the landscape composer to remember that variety is possible in surface, form, materials, color, texture, season, composition and position.

In seeking to vary the surface on which our gardening is to be done, our attention falls first upon the three simplest forms of ground, viz., the plane, the concave and the convex surfaces. And we note also that the concave and convex surfaces give in themselves a much greater variety of view than is afforded by a plane.

This is so potent a fact that in making up the surface of the grounds for park or residence purposes great care is usually taken to avoid a perfect plane, and still to give a uniform swell or depression. Breaking the plane with a succession of little hillocks would be fatal indeed. Of these three classes of surface the concave is usually to be preferred for small areas, for it gives much the best effect of extent. From any point within a concavity the whole surface is visible. This is not true of a convexity; and a perfectly flat surface will, unless given some bold and striking treatment, always have a suggestion of inconsequentiality about it.

A caution needs to be inserted here to secure the best use of these several varieties of surface. As long ago as 1770 Thomas Wheatley said: "In made ground the connection is, perhaps, the principal consideration. A swell which wants it is but a heap; a hollow but a hole; and both appear artificial. . . . Such shapes should be contiguous as most readily unite; and the actual division between them should be anxiously concealed. If a swell descends upon a level; if a hollow sinks from it, the level is an abrupt termination, and a little rim marks it distinctly. To cover that rim a short sweep at the foot of the swell, a small rotundity at the entrance of the hollow, must be interposed." All these cautions are fully worth attention; for the slightest differences in the surface of the ground are obvious and important to the sympathetic beholder.

Broken ground offers an evident and spicy variety. The value of broken ground for developments of the picturesque has already been touched upon.

Sloping grounds have a value all their own, and, for their most effective utilization, require a special treatment. Mr. Parsons, in his "Landscape Gardening," includes a chapter of useful directions for the treatment of such sites, which the student will do well to consult.

Here we will content ourselves by saying that two opportunities are afforded the gardener by sloping grounds which are elsewhere unusual. The first is in the diversity of surface presented. The second is in the advantageous situation for the display of many plants which, in any other position, would not appear to advantage. In respect to the first, it should be explained that even comparatively gentle slopes may be emphasized by proper treatment until they appear to be steep declivities. The first expedient to this end lies in the treatment of the ground itself. It is simply to contrive small irregularities of the surface by placing here and there a little swell which rises abruptly and then falls away very gently down the hill. This part of the declivity will of course be steeper than the general slope; and a few of these contrasts will give the appearance desired. Such variety is often to be sought on a nearly flat and featureless place. A slope also furnishes a specially suitable location for the disposition of rocks, both because they are needed to hold the hillside against washing by rains, and because they appear to much better advantage than on level ground. If the rocks used on a hillside are not in their natural stratifications, and plainly so, they should always be mingled with grass and shrubs and trailing vines. Many trailing vines give great satisfaction if allowed to run at liberty down the side of a bank.*

Water in any form furnishes an ever pleasing addition to a garden, whether as a bubbling fountain, a sparkling brook, or a cool and quiet expanse of mirror-like surface. In brooks and ponds it furnishes one of the most delightful resources of the landscape gardener. Besides the wonderful variety of pleasing effects of which it is in itself capable, it provides the only opportunity

---

* Trailing plants may often be used to great advantage. In many such situations the hardy perennials are especially desirable. See Chap. XXI, Part IV.

VARIETY.

FIG. 14. A GOOD EFFECT OF NATURALNESS.
A specially fine foreground! Prospect Park, Brooklyn, N. Y.

for growing many species and varieties of our most beautiful plants. The possibilities which are open to the landscape gardener in the treatment of water surfaces are so magnificent and manifold that neither description nor enumeration is practicable here. We can only declare with all emphasis that when water surfaces are brought into a landscape composition an immeasurable field of harmonious variety is opened for cultivation by the resourceful gardener.

A curved line changes direction at every point. This is the old definition, which, in itself, is a plain statement that an infinite variety of direction is contained in a curved line. A straight line has only one direction.

The partial concealment of principal points of interest is a common and profitable expedient in most cases,— less so perhaps in the architectural style than in others. In the natural style it is always admissible to group the trees so as to hide, partially or totally, the buildings from most situations, and to give a really complete view from only a few specially favorable points. If a group is so placed as to afford a partial view of the buildings from one standpoint, a totally different view is seen from a second standpoint. In this way the buildings are seen in an endless variety of forms. If a drive or walk leads up to some object of special interest, it may be always considered a good plan, where possible, to give successive glimpses of the object along the way, reserving a full view for a final triumph at a point from which the whole may be best admired.

It is not an uncommon thing at public institutions, where several buildings are needed, to find them all of the same general design and placed in a row, all fronting the same way. I have in mind, as having come within my own observation, two instances of this. One is a large reform school; the other a great state university.

In either case there was room, and to spare, for a difference of design and location. There may be circumstances which make the uniform plan and arrangement the best, but certain monotony is the result.

Deep vistas in any landscape planting are desirable for many reasons. They give depth to the scene. Our gardening is usually on too small a scale to satisfy fully the hungry eye. One's look will wander away and beyond the fence which limits the little garden, and seek to lose itself at the farthest reach of the eyesight's

FIG. 15. THE SKY LINE PROPERLY PUNCTUATED.
Washington Park, Albany.

power. Thus it but satisfies a natural desire if the openings in the garden plantings are so placed as to permit the eye full enjoyment of any good extraneous view. And even within the grounds a long perspective furnishes a variety of views, since in it some objects are seen at a distance, some in middle-ground and some in the foreground.

The sky line should never be monotonous. In speaking of picturesque effects we have already suggested that the sky line should not always be much broken.

The charm of the purely natural style, especially in certain situations, lies in its utter quietness and peacefulness. A horizon full of Lombardy poplar exclamation points is not in unity with such ideas. But the sky line may be diversified more gently. It may be carried high on one side by a mass of heavy woods; it may sink low on another side, to the surface of a lake; and in one or two places it may perhaps be accentuated with the spire-like poplars. This is a matter in which good taste must be exercised; for while very few observers will analyze a scene and itemize the excellencies and defects of the sky line, the most unsympathetic mind may be keenly, though perhaps unconsciously, alive to both.

Very few people have any conception of the multitudinous species and varieties of trees, shrubs, climbers, flowering and foliage plants at the command of the horticultural architect. With twenty sorts of maples, and as many oaks; with poplars in all shapes and sizes; with dozens of varieties of lilacs, scores of spiræas and hundreds of roses; with evergreens and deciduous trees; fastigiate and weeping trees; dark-colored and yellow trees; broad-leaved and cut-leaved trees; big trees and little trees; with other trees, shrubs, climbers and hardy plants literally "too numerous to mention," the gardener need never want for variety of material. To know these resources and to understand the possibilities of each species and variety is to master the landscape gardener's useful alphabet.

"From the artistic point of view, trees have three characteristics which may be separately studied,—form, texture and color."* We have already noticed the general variety in forms available to the landscape gardener; but it is worth while, in the present connection, to emphasize the attractive variety of forms which meet

---

* Mrs. Schuyler Van Rensselaer. "Art out of Doors."

the admiration of the tree lover. The form of a tree is its first and most evident characteristic. Its outline is always beautiful, either in its symmetry or its irregularity, as the case may be; and the man who does not notice the difference between the form of a Sugar maple and a Mossy Cup oak is one to whom l'Angelus might as well have been a chromo.

There are considerable contrasts of color among trees. One may cite as examples the Red oak, the Silver poplar and the Golden willow. But the most pleasing and numerous varieties of color in trees and shrubs are separated from each other as barely distinguishable tints. The proper combination of these tints is delicate work for a sympathetic and artistic mind; but there is, nevertheless, a wide difference between good combinations and bad ones.

The difference between a strip of mosquito netting and a piece of sail cloth is chiefly one of texture. We speak of texture oftenest in connection with woven fabrics, and in that connection we best understand what it means. But it is not a difficult matter to transfer this notion of texture to the apparent solidity, or lack of solidity, in the mass of green which the foliage of any tree may present. A plane tree is not greatly different in form from a Kentucky coffee tree, and yet what a difference in the effect they have on the observer! Compare a catalpa with a honey locust; a tulip tree with a willow. What a difference in the whole aspect of the trees contrasted! These examples may, perhaps, suggest the meaning of Mrs. Van Rensselaer's definition: "By texture of a tree I mean the character of its masses of foliage as determined by the manner of growth of the lighter spray, and the number, shape, disposition and tissue of its leaves." In no other quality of a tree is variety more effective than in the texture. Some striking differences of texture in foliage are shown in Fig. 16.

FIG. 16. DIFFERENCES OF TEXTURE IN FOLIAGE. Central Park, New York.

The horticultural calendar has certain well-marked divisions to which the exhibitor of growing plants may well have thoughtful regard. The first essay that was ever written in the English language on the subject of ornamental gardening opened with an extreme prescription for this arrangement. "I do hold it," says Bacon,* "in the royal ordering of gardens, there ought to be gardens for all the months of the year, in which, severally, things of beauty may be then in season." The essayist proceeds immediately to give a catalogue of the plants seasonable to each month of the year, "for the climate of London." We may doubt whether ten or twelve classes of plants can practicably be made on this basis; but we distinguish in our own æsthetic sensibilities with great differences between spring greens, June roses, midsummer's wealth of foliage, autumn colors and choice winter scenes. Any particular plant is not likely to figure in its perfection through more than one or two of these seasons; and this opens to the landscape gardener a serious problem. The question is, shall we attempt to intermingle the perfections of all the year so as to have somewhat of attractiveness in each several group at all times? Or shall we rather follow the dictum of Lord Bacon, and group together those plants suitable to each successive season? Doubtless each method is at times expedient. If one's garden is so small as to hold only a single group of plants he will scarcely care to buy a single month of superlative perfection at the expense of eleven months of dullness and desolation. But where the gardening is on a more extensive scale the artist may distribute his beauties into any sort of an annual cyclorama which he chooses. He will gain, at all events, a most acceptable variety by having regard to the special seasons mentioned.

---

* **Lord Francis Bacon**, Essays, "Of Gardening."

It is not within the range of our present inquiry to enumerate those special plants which are ready to the gardener's hand for these diverse effects. This has already been done in many useful books, and some suggestions are made in Part III of the present volume. The competent gardener should be able, out of his own knowledge, to select the most pleasing materials for his pictures.

The light gray-greens are perhaps characteristic of the early spring. As trees and shrubs put forth their first unfolding buds the general effect is much different from that given by the same plants after the full dress of foliage is put on. Usually the color is several shades lighter—grayer—and this appearance is further heightened by the grayer twigs not yet covered out of sight but showing more and more dimly through the thickening screen of green leaves. Certain plants are more beautiful in this spring dress than at any subsequent season.

Some of the willows should be prominently mentioned in this category; for example, the Royal willow, *Salix regalis*. Among the smaller flowering plants there is a specially rich field of possibilities, including crocus, narcissus, jonquils, hyacinths, tulips and others. These are suitable not only to be the first occupants of the bleak flower beds after the mulch is removed in the spring, but they should be scattered with a liberal hand through the grass and in the borders, where they come on year after year amid surroundings which make them seem even more dainty and graceful and delightful harbingers of returning spring than when grown in specially prepared beds.

June is the month of roses, brides and college graduates. It is particularly a month of fêtes and of carefree enjoyment of living. Weddings and commencements are the gardener's good patrons, and for them the grounds may well put on their holiday attire. June is the youthful gala time of the garden; and the bold and blushing, smiling and nodding, vain and conscious roses, which would be thought immodest amid the tranquillity of summer or the somberness of autumn, are now received with gladness as the fitting expression of our exuberant emotions. Flowers in abundance, with roses predominating; bright colors and heavy perfumes; with greens and grays and old folks kept in the background—these are the colors for the June picture, the chords for the June music.

In midsummer nothing is more delightful than quiet rest under cooling shade. No flashing colors for us now. No jarring contrasts for the tired eyes. The trees now invite us with their thickest canopy of foliage; and if beneath them stretches a cool, clean greensward, and if the shadows fall all untroubled into a still pool near by, we rest amid these scenes with an overflowing gratitude for the kind hands by which they are provided. We have fled the dusty highway, the burning streets, the noise and hurry and commotion of business. Quiet and solitude are our chief desires. These feelings, common to all men at such times, indicate unequivocally the duty of the gardener. With so unmistakable a demand upon him, he is no gardener at all who will not know what he ought to do.

The beautiful colors of autumn are too much looked upon as secondary qualities of the plants which affect them, and their disposition on the grounds is too much a matter of chance. The gardener ought to recognize in these autumn colors another opportunity for the aggregation of scattered beauties. Through these he may produce one more almost spectacular effect before the winter shuts us all indoors away from the enjoyment of his works. Without speaking of the individual excellencies of the oaks, the liquidambar, the maples and the tulip trees, we may note that two distinct colors appear in great quantities, namely the reds and the yellows. Each of these is present in comparative purity in certain species, and their combination is specially adapted to provide the most extraordinary contrasts. And at no other time of the year would the eye accept such gaudy hues,—no, not even in June,—much less delight in them. But now as our overcoats are buttoned on and

FIG. 17. A WINTER PICTURE.
A sketch of nature's composing.

as we hurry along to get ourselves under shelter from the bustling wind, we are in no mood to note details and examine delicate effects. A picture must cry out after us if it would get our attention. And so the gardener may mass together as much as he pleases of those gorgeous colors of the early frost; and we will stop a moment to admire his work again and to thank him for it ere we betake ourselves to the blazing hearth and the absorbing book.

But even the winter does not wholly rob the gardener of opportunity to please us. Indeed, some of the most gracious products of the ornamental grounds are those blessings which are enjoyed in midwinter. It is a mistake to suppose that the ground must be all bleakness and desolation as soon as snow falls. There is a whole host of the evergreens to refute such a supposition. The variety of them is greater than the uninitiated might at all suspect. With them may be arranged many shrubs and small trees which, though deciduous, have bark of such bright and pleasing hues that they may be shown against dark backgrounds in many cheery combinations. Such are the Golden willow, the Golden spiræa and the Red branched dogwood. A long list of others might easily be made. There are certain corners of the garden which are usually especially conspicuous from the windows of the living rooms; and it is a pity if part of this scene at least cannot be robbed of its winter bleakness and dreariness. If such spots are chosen for beautiful winter effects the designer has gained another triumph in his art.

There is some danger that the beginner in plant grouping will make all his groups alike. This is a very easy thing to do. To avoid it, it first becomes necessary that the operator shall see the sameness into which he is falling. This he can best do in his own work by directing his imagination to construct before him the various finished groups. It is certainly unlikely that the individual plants will be set in exactly homologous positions unless the groups are set with a tape measure. But it is not difficult, if the imagination be serviceable, to compare the probable final effects of two groups, and determine with satisfactory accuracy if the two will look alike twenty years hence. Aside from the ability to see mistakes, it requires an inventive mind to devise new arrangements for groups; but a variety of arrangements they certainly should have in any scheme not intentionally formal.

Single trees or shrubs appear to great advantage when properly placed, and if in all respects good, they add sensibly to the composite beauty of the scene. A single plant will naturally receive more and better attention when standing by itself than though it were in a group with others. For this reason it should have greater individual excellence, if possible. It should be faultless, if that can be. There are many positions about any extensive grounds in which single trees or shrubs will be acceptable units of the composition. The judgment of the designer must point these out; but we may take note that they will usually be comparatively close to the observer, so that the single plants will always be under critical examination. Such places are, then, to be reserved for specially choice specimens. Any rare or remarkable plant,—not monstrous and deformed,—should be given such a place of prominence. And every specimen plant should be remarkable for its individual perfections of good culture.

There are a great many general and common forms given to groups, but their classification and discussion do not belong here. It is sufficient to iterate that this is another point at which conspicuous variety is both possible and proper.

There are, of course, some objects which are seen both near by and at a distance. But in the majority of instances an object,—for instance, a tree,—will be most often seen from the same distance. If it stand at the back of a wood belt, with numerous smaller trees between it and the distant roadway, it may be fairly considered in the background. On the other hand, if it stand close beside a much frequented path or just before the windows of the living room, it is usually seen in the foreground. Between these extremes there is a middleground of greater or less extent. The same plant gives exceedingly diverse effects as seen in these three different positions.

A background is made up most naturally of large trees. Here can be used many species of rough and uncouth growth which would not look respectable at

FIG. 18. BACKGROUND AND SCREEN COMBINED.
Note also the fine grouping of shrubs in the border. Prospect Park, Brooklyn.

close range. Trees of which the texture is so coarse or irregular as to be inadmissible in the foreground, seem at the background to give but a gentle touch to the elsewise unbroken and monotonous surface. Trees of which the colors would jar upon a fastidious eye if seen too close, seem modest and pretty at a greater distance. Moreover, a background must be made up with due thought to the most effectual exhibition of whatever lies between it and the observers. For this reason it must not have a bristling sky line if smooth and roundheaded smaller trees are to appear in front of it. And the opposite mistake must be guarded against. One time with another, the background may best be darker than those groups which intervene between it and the usual point of view. This rule cannot always be adhered to, for it would force all dark colored species out of the fore- and middle-ground; but the reverse presentation must always be looked upon as an undesirable concession to other necessities.

In the foreground, where all plants are under comparatively close scrutiny, only those should be used which will bear such examination. Flowering shrubs and herbaceous plants may be used here. In most cases plants for the foreground must be small; and though we like to have large trees next the walk so that we can enjoy their shade, and though this demand should be met, to a degree, yet a tree so placed adds nothing to the picture, and too many such trees shut off the view entirely. It is a common fault, in the plantings along drives and walks, that they do not give a satisfactory view of the landscape.

There is a great wealth of medium sized trees and large shrubs which look well in middle-ground. Of these are the buckeyes, altheas, lilacs, and the interesting kœlreuteria. The middle-ground is an advantageous place for the exhibition of all tree specimens. If the form of a tree specimen is to be admired it will be put far back in the middle-ground; if it is the beautiful foliage, it will come to the nearer middle-ground. Middle-ground plantings sometimes serve the purposes of background to foreground plantings; but this is not often the case, and it is an undesirable arrangement.

It not infrequently occurs that there are beautiful objects visible from the grounds under treatment and yet lying wholly outside them. It may be mountain scenery, a lake, a view of the ocean, a glimpse of a pretty village, or any other exterior object which bears an interest to the users of the grounds but which is itself wholly beyond the control of the designer. Sometimes these exterior objects are of even greater importance than all the grounds upon which the gardener has to work. This might be the case with a small plot of ground lying next the ocean. In such an extreme case the intelligent gardener will seek to make his entire work contribute to enhance the beauty or effectiveness of the chief though exterior view. This means, of course, that all his effects shall be subordinate to the principal interest. It would be a blameworthy act to place anything in the garden which would draw attention to itself and away from the outside view. In any case he will have careful regard to these exterior views, and will arrange his groupings so as to avail himself of whatever extraneous beauties may be at hand. This, of course, means the leaving of open vistas along well chosen lines. The lines which are thus to be left open, as well as all the long vistas or perspectives which are to be preserved inside the grounds, should be marked first on the engrossed plans, and as the plans are developed on the paper all obstructions may be kept off them. Again, when the plans are being worked out on the grounds these open lines should be carefully marked and the plantings kept from crowding upon them.

CHAPTER VII.

CHARACTER—PROPRIETY.

> Two qualities usually distinguish professional from amateur productions—simplicity and breadth of treatment.
> *Ed. André.*
>
> L'espressione esagerata o negletta constituisce. . . . due difetti oppositi, il barocco, ed il secco o freddo, tra i quali procede amabile la semplicità. *F. Cartolano.*

Character is the most elusive quality of all those with which we deal. Almost all writers on gardening have talked more or less of character, assuming it as a quality, but never approaching a definition or an explanation. Thomas Wheatley did, in fact, long ago introduce a chapter "Of Character" into his remarkably clear analytical outline; but the chapter treated of subjects quite different from those discussed here. If I may venture on the dangerous experiment of a provisional definition, I will say that I intend to suggest by the term character those more delicate distinctions in the general method of treatment, such as may mark one composition from another, even of the same general style. We understand clearly what is meant by character in a man or woman, and I should like to transfer this notion undisturbed to use in the descriptions of gardens. It is a common saying that the face of such and such an acquaintance is pretty but it lacks character. It is perfectly conceivable that a garden might be faultless in the unity and the harmony of its appointments, with everything beautiful and appropriate withal, and yet lack character.

In different words, we might say that character is the personal impress of the designer. Thus we would never expect a poem of pure and lofty character to flow from a wicked heart. We would not expect a painting of great power to originate in a dull, unsensitive mind. No more can we hope to see vigor and dignity displayed in a garden designed by a weak and puerile author. In this close and proper connection of the character of the garden with the character of its designer we may perhaps more clearly understand its present signification.

Certain terms are commonly associated in criticism of gardens, such as simplicity, dignity, boldness, and others. These I take to represent different types of character. I think this is the use commonly made by those who apply them to art compositions, even though those who use them thus have never stopped to generalize under any common term the qualities expressed. These terms, simplicity, dignity and boldness, are sufficiently suggestive of certain characters. This list is not intended to be complete, for, theoretically at least, there may be an indefinite variety of character. The term complexity is added to the list only because it seems to be implied in simplicity. Perhaps elaborateness would be preferred to complexity as a term for a more careful classification.

Between the terms propriety and appropriateness it is hard to choose the better. The latter is the more explicit in its suggestions, but the former has the advantage of brevity and of good associations, which I think ought to be operative in our criticisms of taste in gardening. For as we inquire whether this or that social appointment is marked by strict propriety, so ought we to criticise the items of the gardener's work. It must be said that such criticism is sorely needed, and that many gardeners of some reputation seem never to have reflected that such a test as propriety can be applied to their work. Our American cemeteries are often striking exemplifications of this statement. In them one continually meets objects of such childish conception, such incongruous effect or such gaudy color, as to jar on nerves of any appreciative sensitiveness. Much has recently been said and written on the subject of cemetery ornamentation, and we may assume that we are on the way to inculcate a better taste in this respect. Although every tenent of gardening art is habitually violated in our cemeteries, the most common and disagreeable violations are doubtless instances of disregard for propriety. The matters introduced are not appropriate to the place.

But this is only a single class of improprieties, and is mentioned chiefly for illustration. Propriety is a universal test. Every object and group of objects must submit to it. Thus we would often consider an aviary, or a zoölogical collection, or a suite of dog kennels inadmissible in a garden because they were inappropriate to the surroundings, even though they might be in themselves beautiful and interesting.

I wish to speak here again of a particular class of improprieties to which I have already alluded, namely, the prominent display of monstrous or deformed horticultural specimens. Deformity and monstrosity have a strange fascination to uncultured minds; and there is no more unequivocal testimony to a general poverty of cultivated taste in gardening than the constantly recurring sight of such disfigurements in the gardens of people whose houses are furnished inside with scrupulous taste and propriety. It is surpassingly strange that the city resident, who has room between his house and the street for only a single specimen, will choose for that position the one plant which offers the most blemishes, as though Æsop were better to look upon than Apollo. The commonest vagary of this sort is the little weeping tree, in which the writhing agonies of one monstrous variety are grafted on the top of some straight, courageous stock for better exhibition. As one passes along a residence street in almost any town seeking something in the gardens to admire, how often must he decide that this and that plant was used for its striking incongruities, rather than for its special appropriateness. It seems to the present scribe that propriety is the one thing to be chiefly studied by that large and needy class of Americans who have houses of their own with small grounds attached.

CHAPTER VIII.

FINISH.

> Both richness and polish will, to a certain extent, be the result of keeping. . . . Extreme thinness of plants in beds skirting a lawn, an inferior order of plants in the neighborhood of the house or by the sides of the grass glades, and the use of commonplace or uncongenial ornaments, are inconsistent with richness. *Edward Kemp.*

No one will have read so far as this chapter without having observed the outline which the text attempts to follow. As indicated in that outline, it has been conceived that there are five distinct artistic qualities, in which any ornamental planting may be good or bad. These are unity, variety, character, propriety and finish. These are all in some degree essential; but it will strike the reader at once that they are not all equally important. Those things which are here included under the unsatisfactory term "finish," are not of such paramount and continual necessity as those discussed under unity, for instance. And yet one may understand, without puzzling, that any sort of an art composition may answer all the requirements thus far set forth, and yet fail to yield a due satisfaction because it lacks a painstaking finish. Besides, one may note this defect in the concrete only too easily among pictures, books or landscapes.

In gardening, finish means several things, some of which we may designate here. In the first place, it requires good specimens. All the plants employed must be good of their kind; the minor groups must be good; and the masses must be good. The individual plants must be excellent in proportion to their conspicuousness. If a single specimen of some rare and striking species stand in a prominent place, it cannot be permitted to wear a decrepit, unthrifty, untidy appearance. But besides this, it should have positive excellence to its credit. It should be a plant worth seeing, not merely as a botanical curiosity, but as an example of nature's best work.

Good care is required to keep trees thrifty, to keep plants growing vigorously and luxuriantly. Cultivation and manure are needed. Pruning must be done. Crowded clumps must be thinned out. Sheared trees must be kept sheared, and mowed lawns must be kept mowed. The walks and drives must be kept graded and surfaced and free from weeds. Buildings must be kept painted, and fences put together and standing straight. And dozens of similar matters demand constant attention, or directly the finish of the composition is marred and its whole effectiveness diminished.

Perhaps cleanliness is only a matter of good care; but it sometimes happens that a gardener becomes so absorbed in taking good care of his shrubs and flower beds that he forgets the general cleanliness of his grounds. In public parks the lawns and walks rapidly become littered with papers and rubbish of all sorts, and this may quickly reach such a point as to interfere seriously with the satisfaction of the park habitues. In the farm yard, where good attempts at ornamental gardening are often made, a proper regard for cleanliness would suggest that a wheelbarrow should not be left standing in front of the house unused for a week, and that chicken coops, dog kennels, grindstones and other agricultural paraphernalia should be put behind the main dwelling house, or at least kept off the lawn. On any grounds more or less litter is bound to accumulate, and this may readily amount to enough to spoil the best studied effect of unity, variety, character and **propriety.**

Yet after the landscape gardener has done everything within his power, has gathered the last item of horticultural excellence, and has disposed of it with the artist's happiest effect, he is still dependent, in a very great measure, on the favor of the unmanageable elements for the pleasure he may give his patrons. No one will see a delicately penciled sky line or a softly harmonized background through a blinding dust storm; and a bed of finest roses is apt to look very sorry and drabbled in the midst of a cold rain. Differences in sunshine, light and atmosphere make very surprising differences in the effect of certain views; and as far as possible, all this should be taken into account by the gardener when he makes his plan.

And besides the modifying influence which light and atmosphere exercise on landscape views, they are themselves often a very important part of the picture. Who cares to look at anything else on a day when an early, feathery snow fills the buoyant atmosphere with a delightful, softening, luminous, hush-compelling haze? And sometimes there are clouds and a sunset as beautiful as the woods or as sublime as the ocean. These do not belong to the gardener, but they may fit into his picture, and enhance the pleasure which it gives; and shall he not appropriate whatever of them he can? Everyone knows that the landscape painter spends his chiefest pains to give accurate representations and stirring suggestions of light and atmosphere; but the landscape gardener has the real commodities in unmeasured, ever-shifting variety. Let him make all possible use of them, and if the elements are commonly unpropitious, as they are in some countries, he may have his proper doubts about the practicability of undertaking any gardening plans at all. Fortunately almost every country, whatever its shortcomings, has some good qualities of climate which may be studied and turned to advantage.

PART III.

General Problems.

CHAPTER IX.

ENTRANCES, DRIVES AND WALKS.

> For an approach to be good there must be an easy turn-in from the high road; the grade within the gate must be as uniform and as gentle as possible; there must be no sharp turns; . . . the house must be well displayed to advancing eyes; and the line of gravel must not so intersect the ground as to interfere with a beautiful arrangement of its parts, or to be itself a disagreeable object when seen from the house. *Mrs. Van Rensselaer.*

The orator takes great pains that his exordium shall be at once a fitting introduction to his oration and calculated to win the favor of his audience. The composer of an opera gives special care to his overture, endeavoring to introduce the best themes of the subsequent score, and to make an agreeable impression on his hearers. In the same way, when a landscape gardener plans a considerable picture he tries to arrange it so that the approaching visitor shall get not only a prejudice in its favor, but also a fair suggestion of its character. Among farmers who try to arrange their homes tastefully, and among people who have summer residences in the country, the importance of an appropriate approach is quite generally felt. In some other lines of work,—park-making, for example,—it is sometimes underestimated.

When the grounds are of any considerable size there ought to be an adequate (undefined) entrance area. The entrance is of some importance in itself, and other items in its immediate neighborhood may best be made subordinate to it. Usually this area will be more or less enlarged by being recessed from the outside. This emphasizes the entrance, makes it seem more hospitably inviting, gives room for a carriage turn, etc. Usually there will be a gateway of some sort; and if the vicinity, outside or inside, is full of buildings, the design of the entrance will probably be architectural in its main features. There is such an infinite variety of architectural ideas to be worked out for such places that no general suggestions can be made. For country places, where the entrance is made among purely natural surroundings, considerably less of architectural effect is permissible. Some very simple, substantial stone work is usually best. Downing, and the people of his day, always affected "rustic" work—poles with the bark on—for such places; and though these sometimes give a satisfactory result they are much less in vogue at the present.

FIG. 19. STREET ENTRANCE.
Destination unrevealed.

It is quite customary to make the turn-in, especially on moderate sized places, at right angles with the exterior highway. While this arrangement is often best, it might be greatly improved, in many cases, by substituting a less abrupt turn. The main drive may frequently be arranged to leave the public way very gently at an acute angle.

From the entrance to the house or other main point of interest the drive should proceed as directly as possible, and still be gracefully curved. Its course and direction will be modified chiefly by the contour of the ground. Sharp elevations or depressions must be alike avoided, by carrying the drive around them; but the grade of the drive must be compromised sometimes with the course to be adopted, and nothing will take the **place of good judgment** in doing this. The curve should be gentle and not winding. It should reveal something new at each turn. The best view of the house should be carefully treated. Its own effect should be reserved to it, and not squandered on a half dozen unimpressive and inadequate views. If the drive gives one good view, the poor views ought to be hidden by plantings or by the course of the road.

For very large and stately mansions, or in comparatively small grounds, the approach may be straight and lead directly to the front of the main building. Such an arrangement lends dignity to a building which is in itself imposing. Such an avenue of approach is usually planted with rows of trees. Other drives, besides the

FIG. 20. ENTRANCE TO A MILITARY PARK, VERMONT.

main approach, may be treated in the same general way as walks.

Walks and subsidiary drives must be provided where people want to walk or where they expect to drive. Neither is artistic in itself. Every foot of walk or drive is a trouble, an expense, and usually a distinct detraction from the artistic beauty of the place. They should, then, be designed to fit the actual demands of traffic about the place. The most practicable thing is often to await the most explicit call for a walk. When a path begins to appear through the grass, the need of a walk is manifest and its general direction pretty accurately indicated.

Gentle curves are better than straight lines, for walks, except upon small places or in a geometrical plan. These curves must be determined by the exercise of good taste and judgment, on the ground. A design made on paper is apt to be very unsatisfactory when transferred to the soil, unless it is made by an experienced hand from an accurate topographical survey. Even then it may not fit. Curves made up of arcs of circles are not very satisfactory, unless the arcs are comparatively short and judiciously combined. If a road is properly made, only a very short arc will be visible from any point; and this enables the designer, when working on the ground, to make many curves and combinations of curves which would be decidedly unpleasing when accurately platted on a map.

When a walk or a drive branches, each arm should take such a course as to appear to be the proper contin-

FIG. 21. DIVERGING DRIVES.
a, Correct. b, Wrong.

uation of the trunk. Imagine how one arm would look with the other removed. Would it still be complete? Would the whole seem to be the perfectly natural course for the walk? Such bifurcations should not be at too obtuse an angle; and yet this angle of divergence is of quite minor importance if the foregoing consideration is kept fully in mind.

Where several drives or walks meet, upon demand, a suitable concourse must be provided, for at such points there is always apt to be a congestion of traffic. The size and form of this concourse is determined solely by circumstances. Sometimes such a spot commands some specially fine view. The place may be treated, then, with direct regard to the outlook. When no desirable external view is to be exhibited, the concourse area may have a special treatment of its own. It may be flanked by heavy plantings on part of its circumference, with open vistas left at the most favorable points. Or, if near a building, as is frequently the case, it may be treated as an outlying part of the architect's work, and made to conform to it in shape and ornamentation.

Walks must be well drained, but should not rise above the adjacent soil surface. Neither should they be depressed much, if any, below it, except for the necessary gutter at the edges. The practical construction of walks and drives is a matter of immense importance, but it belongs rather to engineering than to landscape gardening, and besides, there is not room here for a discussion of it. The principal artistic demands have, however, been pointed out.

CHAPTER X.

THE PLANTING OF STREETS AND AVENUES.

> The villages of New England, looking at their sylvan charms, are as beautiful as any in the world. Their architecture is simple and unpretending,—often, indeed, meager and unworthy of notice. The houses are surrounded by inclosures full of trees and shrubs, with space enough to afford comfort, and ornament enough to denote taste. But the main street of the village is an avenue of elms, positively delightful to behold. Always wide, the overreaching boughs form an aisle more grand and beautiful than that of any old Gothic cathedral. —*A. J. Downing.*

We have already alluded to the treatment of streets, saying that streets and avenues, since they manifestly follow geometrical lines, demand a formal treatment. And this formality ought to go further than the mere alignment of the trees. It is still more important that the various trees should be of the same species and of the same age and uniformly developed. Not enough pains is commonly taken to secure these desiderata. One can easily satisfy himself by his own observations anywhere in the United States that, while street trees are nearly always planted in orderly rows, it is the somewhat rare exception to find a row of really good and uniform specimens. Such uniformity is not easy to secure, especially when its importance is not understood at the outset. The only advice which can be given is to exercise great care in planting and the utmost vigilance during the early years of development.

An explanation of frequent cases of unsatisfactory growth of young street trees is to be sought in the inadequate feeding given them. If they grow close to the street on one side and to a paved walk **or row of build-**

ings on the other, their roots must of course ramify for many feet underneath these surface obstructions. Aside from this the soil is apt to be of the poorest. It is hardly to be expected, in such circumstances, that a thrifty growth can be secured without something being done to offset these drawbacks. Liberal supplies of fertilizers, especially potash salts and nitrates, ought to be worked into the soil whenever the surface is accessible.

It is a good plan to set street trees rather close together in the beginning, and to thin them as they grow and begin to crowd. This plan, however, demands very conscientious attention to the thinning, for sometimes it is a matter of considerable heroism to cut out strong, thrifty trees along the avenue when they are only beginning to crowd their neighbors just a little. But any undue procrastination is sure to damage the survivors very seriously.

The distance between trees in the row will be influenced somewhat by the width of the street. In a wide street, where there is room enough for the full development of each tree, they will be planted farther apart. If the street is wide enough, the trees should always stand between the walk and the curb. It is wide enough if, from curb to curb, the width is one and a half times the distance recommended for the trees in the rows. On a narrower street, trees should stand between the walk and the buildings or should be dispensed with. There are many beautiful streets in this country which support four rows of trees. Such streets should have the central avenue twice as wide as the distance between trees in the row; and the distance between the two rows on either side should be somewhat less than that between trees.

If, now, we are seeking a formal effect in our rows of street trees, it follows that this effect will be emphasized by trees which naturally assume somewhat formal

FIG. 22. A WELL PLANTED STREET.
Royal Palms, near Havana.

shapes. It will not do to press this point too far, but it should have careful thought. We have all seen strikingly beautiful rows of the very formal Lombardy poplar, and the effect of dignity given by an avenue of palms leaves an impression not to be forgotten.

The American elm is doubtless the commonest street tree in America. It has many undeniably good qualities to recommend it. The grounds about Harvard and Yale could not possibly spare their rows of elms, and there are hundreds of other streets in all parts of the country which would be desolate indeed if all the elms had to go. And yet there are serious objections to the elm as a street tree, besides the fact that it is often defoliated by caterpillars of various species, as, indeed, are many other trees. The elm varies greatly in size and form, and it is almost impossible to find a long street of old elms which does not suffer from the sad lack of uniformity which this variability introduces. The elm is, also, one of the least formal of our trees, and so detracts from the unity of the geometrical idea in street planting. It would be silly to advise planters to discard the elm altogether; but it will not be too much to suggest that some other species should always be duly considered.

The maples are excellent street trees, especially the sugar maple, and many admirable examples of their effectiveness are to be found in the northern states. The sugar maple is a strong, healthy grower, with a regular, clear-cut outline, and has the advantage of a very tidy appearance through the winter months. In southwestern states the soft maple, or silver maple (*Acer dasycarpum*), takes the place of the sugar maple, but is not so good a tree.

The American sycamore is one of our finest street trees in many situations. Anyone who does not know how beautiful this species is should study the effects **pro-**

duced by it in Washington, especially in the magnificent avenues just west of the Capitol. The sycamore does not succeed north of Massachusetts and central New York, but for the greater part of the United States it is worth careful consideration.

Other species which are sometimes used with happy results are honey locust, Kentucky coffee tree, pines and spruces. There is a most striking and beautiful avenue of ginkgo trees in Washington leading to the Department of Agriculture; and there are some pretty rows of ailanthus about the Temple square in Salt Lake City. Occasionally one will find an avenue of oaks, and if it is a good one there are few trees more satisfactory. Poplars, especially the cottonwood, are used in the trans-Mississippi states, but they are usually a poor makeshift. It is always very gratifying to find a good street of trees of an unusual species, and this is a thing which the street makers might well hold in remembrance.

CHAPTER XI.

WATER, AND ITS TREATMENT.

> The water surfaces of a park need more study and care to make them appear natural in outline than does the general ground surface of the park. — *John C. Olmsted.*
>
> Spaces of clear surface among water plants, with undisturbed reflections, are particularly necessary to secure the best effects. — *Samuel Parsons, Jr.*

The artistic possibilities of any place are almost doubled with the introduction of a fair amount of water surface. Water gardening gives room for almost as rich a variety of plants and plant combinations as does the open ground. There are still ponds, broad reaches of river, trickling brooks, playing fountains, and many other general forms of expression which water may assume; and in each case new opportunities are offered to the plant lover.

The water itself is one of the most effective elements of any picture. A painted landscape is hardly complete without a touch of water somewhere. And a public park would probably be considered seriously deficient without some kind of a lake. The restful and quieting influences of rural scenery are peculiarly enhanced by stretches of still water. The very best effect is gained when the grounds are so fortunately situated as to give a good view of a long reach of river, or a broad lake, or of the ocean. This consideration is so cogent as to determine the location of a very large proportion of summer residences. They seem to be gregarious along the seaside and on all the lake shores. This effectiveness of water pictures rests upon a primitive human instinct which has been strengthened rather than

82   LANDSCAPE GARDENING.

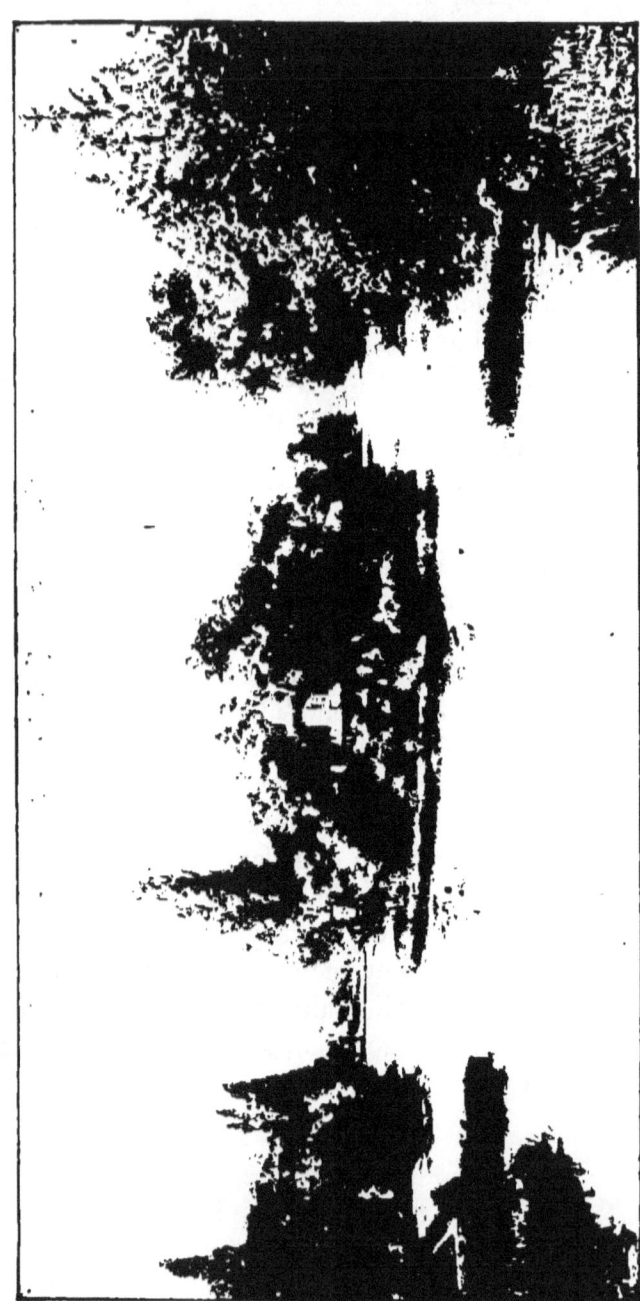

FIG. 23. THE EFFECTIVE USE OF WATER.
Grand Lac, Bois de Boulogne, Paris. Note also the excellent sky line.

impaired by the conventions of civilization. For every reason, then, stress must be laid upon the value of such water views. They must be sought, preserved and sympathetically displayed.

When the point of view is at the water's edge the water forms the entire picture,—excepting, of course, the background of trees or mountains which may be beyond it. But when, as usual, the house, or the path, or the drive is some distance from the shore, the treatment of the intervening foreground becomes a delicate and important matter. The gardener who would plant a coleus bed on the sea beach would properly be sent to the insane asylum; but any other gaudy or trivial piece of work put into the foreground would be as inexcusable. To give the water best effect the space between it and the observer should be obstructed the least possible. Usually it will be in grass. It will be only moderately undulating. A perfectly flat surface and broken ground are equally to be avoided. The view should then be set off at the sides by large trees, if possible. Nothing else answers quite so well. If they can be arranged so as to be seen in a long and varied perspective, they will be the more satisfactory. It is impossible to give an exact prescription for the treatment of all such cases, for a good result depends on the tasteful management of delicate details; and yet, in the greater number of these very common water views, the landscape gardener has choice of only a limited number of devices, the principal considerations of which have here been pointed out.

The small pond, comprehended entirely within the grounds under treatment, offers quite another series of problems. If it is large enough to give some pictorial effect, there will naturally be arranged a series of glimpses and completer views from various advantageous points, mostly near its banks. These will, however, be

LANDSCAPE GARDENING.

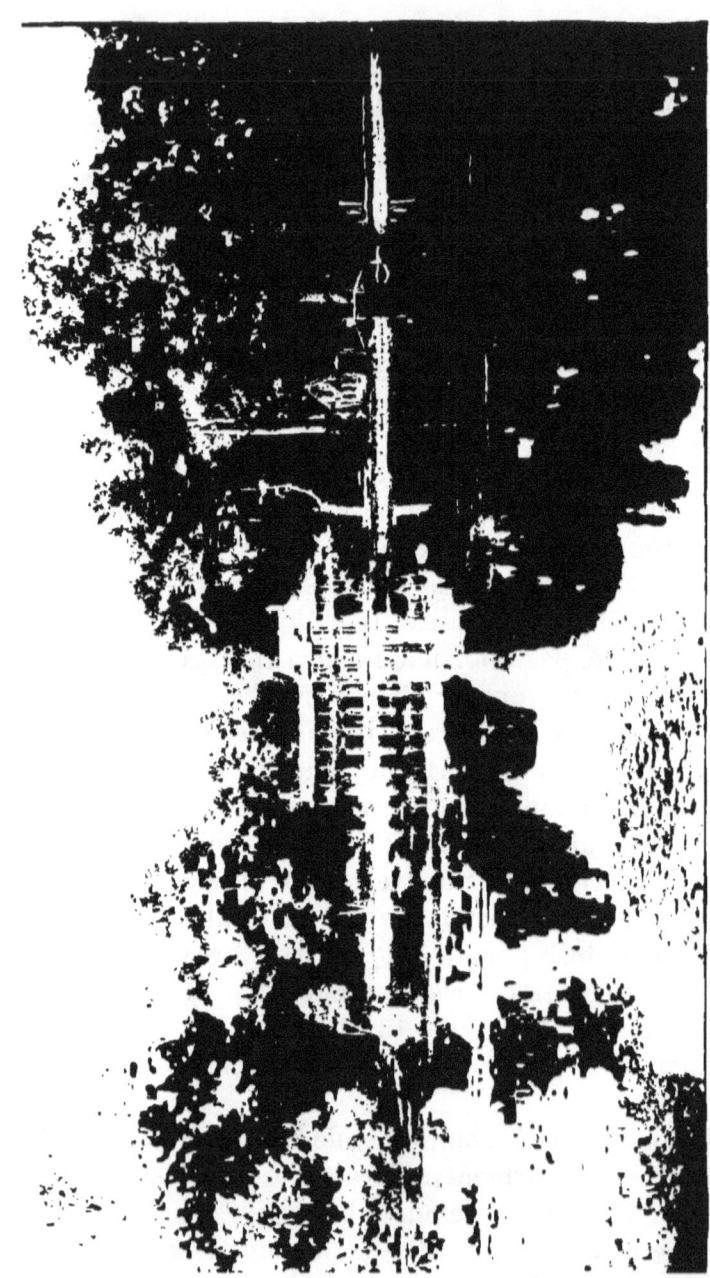

FIG. 24. THE WATER MIRROR. A fine sheet of water, with excellent plantings in the background. Trianon, Paris.

chiefly glimpses, and are to be treated accordingly,—not with the same dignity and seriousness which are given to larger views, though in general the plan of treatment will be a sort of miniature of that already described.

Besides this, the small pond offers wonderful opportunities for planting. Sedges, cat-tails, lotuses, water lilies, alders and many other plants are especially suitable to the banks and shallow water of ponds. Very fine effects can be arranged with them. The outline of a pond may be tastefully broken, so that what would otherwise look like a mere cup in the ground becomes a necessary and integral part of the whole composition. The grass should come down to the water in places. In other parts a fringe of overhanging alders may form the outline. Still further along the sedges and cat-tails may jut far out into the still water. It is hard to spoil such a picture.

If some of the trees along the pond shore are situated so as to cast their reflections upon the water, their effect will be more than doubled. Everyone knows what a pleasing touch such reflections give to a picture. But the trees must not be of the unquiet sort, like some of the willows, always shivering and shimmering in the breeze, for the pond must be still and the images on its surface must be still. It is the quietness and peacefulness of such a picture which attract us, and we are very sensitive of even the slightest interference. And yet some of the statelier willows, especially the heavier weeping willows, make excellent pond borders. Ash trees, and sycamores with thorns, and viburnums, and many more such things, enter helpfully into such effects.

The small rivulet does not seem to enjoy the favor which its comparative merits would justify. It cannot become a part of the same sedate and serious pictures which depend so much on large sheets of water; but it has an equal degree of efficiency in its own way. When

FIG. 25. BACK-YARD GARDEN IN A CITY LOT. DAYTON, OHIO.

the landscape approaches that character which **André** calls "gay,"* nothing can be more appropriate than the glancing, glimmering, vanishing, changing glimpses of running water in a small brook. Such a brook should be wooded, and among the trees should be loose tangles of vines, shrubbery, brambles and brakes. Rocky impediments in the bed of the brook, if the character of the ground will justify them, give little, tinkling cascades where the sunlight flashes. Here and there a calmer pool may grow some rushes or lily pads. And every turn gives a change of view, and every change of view a new delight.

A good brook offers, indeed, a multitude of opportunities for delightful landscape gardening. It is unfortunate that such opportunities are sometimes wholly neglected.

---

* "Le genre gai ou riant. . . . s'applique généralement à des scènes champêtres, pastorales, doucement animées, variées, qui constituent la grande majorité des cadres dans lesquels le talent du dessinateur est appelé à s'exercer."—André, L'Art des Jardins, 138.

CHAPTER XII.

THE CITY OR SUBURBAN LOT.

> The fact is, the easiest way to spoil a good lawn is to put a flower bed on it; and the most effective way to show off flowers to least advantage is to plant them in a bed in the greensward.
> *L. H. Bailey.*

In the planting of city and suburban residence grounds there seems to be the largest field for improvement in this country. One sees in such places more exhibitions of execrable bad taste than anywhere else, to be sure; but such things indicate the willingness and the energy to do something, and taste often improves as work goes on. Those people who own their grounds in the towns and suburban districts are the truest home lovers in the nation; and as a class they have the means, the desire and the taste,—often uneducated in this particular line,—for home improvement. Still there is much too little done in the way of gardening or of any tasteful amelioration of the grounds.

While the housebuilder gladly puts $3,000 or $20,000 into his house, he regards $50 or $100 as ample outlay for the ornamentation of the surrounding grounds. And while he is sure to employ an architect and pay him $100 to $500 for planning the house, he does not think of consulting a landscape gardener to design the surfacings and plantings, but leaves such things to the cheap day laborer who mows the lawn or takes care of the stable. These things make it obvious that the gentle art of gardening has not yet gained a proper appreciation from all those who should be its votaries.

The first great question to be decided, in laying out the grounds of a moderate-sized city home, is whether a fine effect from the street shall be sought, or a comfortable outdoor privacy be secured to the residents. On large grounds both these desiderata may be secured; but on small lots one must be sacrificed. The good, old fashioned English style of securing privacy in small places,—a method adopted by many citizens of a former period in America,—is to have a thick, high hedge all along the front. One still sees numbers of such hedges of arbor vitæ, or privet, or mulberry, completely screening the house and grounds from the street. Such an arrangement has its very simple and substantial advantages, and if it is to be adopted there is no further advice to be given, except to choose a thrifty species for the hedge and keep it cleaned and well pruned.

A practicable modification of this method, but one not often seen, is to plant a somewhat irregular screen of mixed trees and shrubs and herbaceous materials. Such a screen can be arranged in the same general way as an ordinary border planting, except that it will usually face in two directions. This will shield the company on the lawn from the passers along the street, and will, at the same time, give opportunity for the introduction of an indefinite variety of ornamental plants, some of which are visible from the street and some from the house and lawn.

But a great many people do not live much on the lawn, or prefer for other reasons to make the grounds a setting for the house in such a way that the whole shall give the best possible effect from the street. In such cases there come into play all the principles of taste which govern gardening anywhere. As in other gardening operations, unity is most to be regarded. It is often violated to excess. Many city gardens are only aggregations of unrelated and incompatible features picked up here and yonder because they struck the passing fancy of the collector. A good plan should be made and fol-

90   LANDSCAPE GARDENING.

FIG. 26. THE PRIVACY OF THE HOME GARDEN.
A picture of comfort from the most inexpensive materials.

lowed. This plan should be upon very simple lines,— the simpler as the grounds are smaller. It is here, more than elsewhere, imperative that the center of the lawn in front of the house be kept open. If the grounds are small, the space will seem to be increased by placing the house at one side and comparatively far from the street. And then, if it may be done without sacrificing the appearance of directness, the front walk may also be carried to one side, leaving the main lawn intact and very much augmented in its apparent extent. The plantings are then made in irregular borders along the sides of the lot and at the back, with more or fewer herbs and shrubs and climbers against the porches and the foundations of the house itself, according to its architectural character. Mistakes specially to be avoided in such a scheme of treatment are formal flower beds in the lawn, detached shrubs, horticultural monstrosities of all sorts, conspicuous edgings along walks, noticeably imperfect specimens of any kind, etc.

So far we have considered the treatment of the city residence lot in accordance with the natural style of gardening. Circumstances are often such as to make a geometrical treatment even more desirable. In fact, the tendency in this country is so strong toward the natural method of planting that many excellent opportunities for fine effects in the opposite method are ignored. The prospective planter of small grounds, who has not yet formed decided preferences for the natural style, is strongly recommended to bring himself to the clearest possible appreciation of the beauties and capabilities of the geometrical style before he commits himself to any particular plan.

In treating the small city lot according to the formal style, the ground is first laid out in purely geometrical lines. There are straight walks, and rectangular or circular areas for grass or plants; **and if terraces are** necessary, they are laid out so that their lines form a part of the general framework. Then the hedges which are to be clipped, the formal flower beds, and the other accessories of this style of gardening are filled in upon the plan, according to the principles laid down in Chapter III.

Special caution must be given the suburban resident and amateur gardener against planting too much of too many things. Everyone knows how easy it is to over-furnish a room; but few realize how much easier it is to over-furnish a lawn. The flower-loving suburban gardener wants everything in the nurseryman's catalog; and such an appetite is a blessing only when properly restrained. Perhaps it will be an acceptable hint to say that more things may be grown in tasteful arrangement within a small compass by close planting of herbaceous or semi-herbaceous annuals and perennials in irregular borders, than by any system of bedding or nursery crowding such as is commonly practiced on small places. Many diverse sorts of plants thus forced into company give a fine example of the universal struggle for existence, and of the mutual adaptations to which such an encounter gives rise. The nasturtiums will clamber up the strong stems of the sunflowers; the petunias will look out from under the castor beans, and the verbenas from under the petunias; the yellow coreopsis will mingle freely with the blue pentstemons, and over all will tower the hollyhocks, the heleniums and the rudbeckias. Give them plenty of food, an abundance of water, and constant, sympathetic interest, and how they will grow, and what a jolly place it will be! This is where many a successful business man recruits, all summer long, his flagging energies by daily relaxation among his shrubs and flowers and family.

CHAPTER XIII.

THE ORNAMENTATION OF FARMYARDS.

> We would have the cottage, the farmhouse and the larger country house, all marked by a somewhat distinctive character of their own, so far as relates to making them complete and individual of their kind; and believing, as we do, that the beauty and force of every true man's life or occupation depend largely on his pursuing it frankly, honestly, openly, with all the individuality of his character, we would have his house and home help to give significance to, and dignify, that daily life and occupation, by harmonizing with them. For this reason we think the farmer errs when he copies the filigree work of the retired citizen's cottage, instead of showing that rustic strength and solidity in his house which are its true elements of interest and beauty.
> *A. J. Downing.*

Everyone must some time have felt a shock at coming upon a city house in the country. Such houses are, fortunately, rare; but they are not unknown. There will be the house of complicated architecture, with gables, and porticoes and loggias, and porte-cochère; and there will be all the other accompaniments to give a thoroughly urban air to the whole place. And most persons will feel instinctively what an impropriety such a composition presents. The country house must have a thoroughly rural air. The owner has hardly the choice of any other plan. And to give a rural atmosphere some sort of naturalistic treatment of the grounds will be necessary.

This naturalistic treatment, on account of the considerations already hinted at, ought to be on a comparatively large scale. This is usually possible, for the farm can commonly spare whatever room is required for the homestead and its immediate dependencies. In those rather too common cases in which the house and gardens are of mean extent or are crowded into the highway, the trouble has arisen, not through parsimony of room, but simply through thoughtlessness of the needs of the farm home. A farmhouse ought to have plenty of room; and if the grounds have already been laid out so as not to leave ample space, the best thing that can be done is to reconstruct them altogether, or so far as may be necessary to gain a free and roomy farmyard.

A farmhouse ought to be comparatively remote from the road. The distance will vary according to the hight of the house, the slope of the land, the taste of the builder, and other circumstances; but the distance ought not to be less than three times the hight of the house, or more if the ground slopes upward from the street. If the house is put some distance back into the grounds, as is sometimes very desirable, and has an approach of its own, the main view of the house ought still to be given at a distance something greater than three times the hight of the house.

This is not a work on architecture, but it may not be out of place to make a few brief suggestions respecting the farmhouse itself. Generally some very simple plan of architecture is to be preferred. A sharp or much broken roof is especially to be avoided. Porches ought to be wide, and their floors not high from the ground, especially if the place be level. City dwellers affect high porches and second-story balconies for the sake of the privacy they give; but privacy is more easily secured on a farm. Country houses are often painted white, and sometimes the result is fairly agreeable. Usually some other color will give a better effect, however,—some slaty, or grayish, or other neutral shade,— for white surfaces mar the rurality of the general effect.

A farmyard without some large shade trees is a very unsatisfactory affair. This needs hardly to be mentioned. The more common evil is an over-indulgence of this craving for shade trees; and there are many houses badly shadowed and shut in, and many yards cramped and crowded by twice or thrice the number of large trees which the place ought to support. The ax is the remedy for such cases. The remedy is, indeed, very hard to apply to trees which have become old friends, but the improvement will be worth all the sorrow which comes with it. The best way of all is to make such thinnings very much earlier in the development of the

FIG. 27. SUGGESTION FOR A FARMYARD.
a a a, Sugar maples; *b b*, shrubbery; *c*, climbers on porch; *d*, hawthorn; *e e*, elms; *f*, basswood or horse-chestnut; *g g*, sycamores.

grounds, and then there is likely to be much less grief in the family.

To produce the rural, naturalistic effect here recommended, there should be a liberal use of shrubs. And for the most part, the common native shrubs of the woods and fields are much superior to the finest exotics. Those things which are so common as to be slightingly passed by are often the very best. Buck-berries, snowberries, alders, elders, dogwoods, wild roses, the flowering raspberry, and many others which are always ready to the hand, should be planted in profusion. If they prove to be too thick, they may be thinned out as they grow; but it is very seldom that such a necessity arises. Of course, many of the nurseryman's shrubs are well worth having, and may be added as occasion requires and means permit.

In connection with shrubs, a great many hardy perennials may be used to advantage. These are more fully discussed in another place. Annual flowering plants are not very useful or appropriate in the ordinary front yard, though they may be grown in any quantity in the side borders if desired. Such flowering plants are usually grown for the blossoms themselves rather than for anything they contribute to the general effect; and their end is then best served if they can be cultivated in a separate garden plot, behind the house or at one side, enclosed somewhere, or in connection with the kitchen garden. In this latter situation they are likely to receive better culture and more fertilizer, and to give correspondingly larger crops of finer blossoms.

A fence about the farmyard is frequently a positive necessity, but it need not be a whitewashed picket fence. The less conspicuous it be, the better; and some sort of hedge, of arbor vitæ, holly, privet, or similar materials, is much to be preferred. The plan shown in Fig. 27, for a farmyard, is offered merely as a suggestion, and should not be copied. The chief features to which attention should be directed are the open space in front of the house, the limited number of large trees, and the shrubbery at the sides.

CHAPTER XIV.

THE AMELIORATION OF SCHOOL GROUNDS.

> We have an ideal picture, that refreshes our imagination, of common schoolhouses scattered all over our wide country, not wild bedlams which seem to the traveler plague spots on the fair country landscape, but little nests of verdure and beauty; embryo Arcadias, that beget tastes for lovely gardens, neat houses and well cultivated lands.
>
> *A. J. Downing.*

It would seem as though the grounds about a school building stood in special need of such means of refinement as trees and shrubs. But we know how often, especially in the cities, they have not the room even for green grass.

But supposing we have one of those fortunate suburban or rural schools, whose founders have had the foresight and the benevolence to reserve for it some more adequate grounds, what can we do in the way of ornamentation? Obviously, fancy gardening with expensive plants is out of the question. Something simple must be undertaken, and usually something inexpensive. If the circumstances of soil and climate and the attendance of the school will permit its maintenance, a good turf is most to be desired. But in many places this will be tramped to pieces; and then some sort of paving ought to be provided,—gravel, or sand or stone.

If a school yard can have a few large trees they will always be greatly prized by everyone. Their value is so great that, in places having the room, very considerable pains should be taken to supply them. Usually it is best to plant the largest trees possible. Thousands of our American schools celebrate an Arbor day. Usually the trees planted on such occasions are considerable in number, put inconsiderable in size. Most of them succumb to various casualties before the end of term time, and the remainder die of neglect during vacation. If the same work were applied to the planting of one or two large trees,—twelve, fifteen or twenty feet high, with sufficiently good roots,—the chances of success, under the circumstances, would be greater.

Shrubs can be used to advantage on school grounds along back boundaries, especially against fences. Good, thrifty native species, like dogwood, hawthorn, and even the wild bramble, will add greatly to the looks of the premises by relieving them of that cheerless, depressing barrenness which too commonly characterizes the schoolhouse lot. Attention will need be given that such shrubbery borders do not become unsightly by the accumulation of litter, but no other special care or cultivation will be required.

One often hears it argued, how nice and proper it would be to grow flowering plants and plants of economic interest on the school grounds. There is a very sufficient multitude of reasons why this is seldom possible, but the idea is admirable and one to be encouraged. If such good things seem to be within reach, the garden beds will best be put along the back and side borders. It is possible in such situations, and under favorable conditions, to cultivate narrow beds, laid out in a manner to be out of the way of most of the romping play which occupies the main grounds. But for all such plantings the hardy perennials are to be recommended above the annuals, other things being equal.

The great difficulties in the way ought not to deter school boards, teachers and patrons from using their best efforts to ameliorate, as much as possible, the uninviting blankness of the ordinary school grounds, especially in view of the very manifest desirability of such improvement.

CHAPTER XV.

SOMETHING ABOUT PUBLIC PARKS.

> Contact with and contemplation of natural scenery, especially of pastoral scenery, bring positive refreshment to the mind. Green pastures and still waters now, as in the days of the Hebrew poet, restore the soul. This is a fundamental truth, and, therefore, it has profound practical importance. — *W. A. Stiles.*
>
> It is a mistake to suppose that the value of charming natural scenery lies wholly in the inducement which it presents to a change of mental occupations, exercise and air-taking. Besides and above this, it acts in a strictly remedial way to enable men to resist the harmful influences of ordinary town life. . . . It is thus a sanative agent of vital importance. — *F. L. Olmsted.*

There seems to be a very considerable misapprehension and inappreciation of the uses of a public park. In fact, a majority of people would probably say, if pressed to express their true feelings, that, personally, they could do very well without the parks. Parks and public gardens are generally felt to be a luxury, and suitable for the edification chiefly of people of leisure. On second thought, however, anyone must see the mistakenness of such views, though it is still very difficult to demonstrate the practical utility of public parks to the skeptic.

First of all, city parks have been likened to lungs, which help to purify the air and so make breathing less hazardous. Those who know how difficult it is in the city to get pure water or pure air will know how real such a benefit is. Perhaps the country visitor, who is used to clean air with plenty of oxygen in it, is most oppressed by the snuffy, dusty, filthy stuff he has to breathe when occasionally he comes to town. But such air is doubtless quite as harmful to those who are accustomed to it as to those who notice it more. It must be regarded as a prolific source of disease. Such air, however, when it has room to circulate, purifies itself with comparative rapidity; and the usefulness of even a small open space may extend to a considerable circumference.

The public park offers the only outdoor recreation room for very large numbers of city dwellers. This is not the place, nor is it necessary here, to argue that the hurried, worried city population stands in great need of such rest and recreation. It may be regarded as self-evident. One who looks about in any city park on any reasonably fair day will find how large a number of people have felt such a need; and he is much more likely to conclude that hundreds of others should have come to the park, than to think that those whom he sees have no business there. If one thinks about such things while he is in the park and sees the mothers with their babies, the girls and boys picnicking, the young people on their bicycles, the families in carriages, and the hundreds of others of every age and estate relaxing from the stress of ordinary care, he must conclude that these people get some good out of it, which, in the sum total, makes a rich interest on the park investment.

By far the most important purpose which the park serves, however, is that of mental sanitation. The merest novice in city living knows how wearing upon the mind, and upon the nerve centers generally, are the din and hurry and unrest from which no one has immunity. When continually exposed to such conditions, the mind and the senses become dulled and dimmed by the multitude of offensive impressions which they are obliged to bear. The senses need rest and the mind needs renovation. The man who does not bathe his body once a week is not thought respectable; yet no one blames him for letting his intellect go uncleansed for the space of a year. But as the mind responds much more quickly than the body to its environment, it demands the more frequent and thorough restoration. Many minds need thorough ablution,—disinfection. Every mind needs frequent rest and clarification. For these purposes nothing is better than rural scenery, quiet, and clean air. The quiet woodland shade, the cool greensward, the budding and blossoming flowers, have a powerfully refreshing influence which is felt by everyone, but underestimated by most of us. The problem of modern city life seems to be less the development of bodily perfections, than keeping the mind keyed up to the highest point of efficiency; and in the solution of that problem the open park ground must always prove a very important quantity.

If, now, we inquire how the best artistic effect is to be realized in the development of municipal parks, we have opened a most difficult and important question. Under the usual democratic method of management, an artistic success is in the highest degree improbable. We have already familiarized ourselves, in a previous chapter, with the primacy of the demand for unity in landscape composition. We have seen how necessary it is that one mind, disembarrassed of all extraneous influences, shall create one coherent plan which shall ever after be strictly followed. And yet the ordinary way is to do these things by legislation! Even after a park is fully established in some fair degree of completeness it must still suffer alterations with each change in the board of aldermen.

All this is not meant as an argument against democratic city government, but to point out clearly the tremendous difficulty of securing good landscape gardening in public parks, and to show how imperative it is that every means be taken to secure continuity and stability of park management. There is, of course, no argument to be brought against the demands of "practical politics;" but in those cases, not unknown, where common sense still has a hearing, there is yet hope for an intelligent treatment of this important question. There are places in this country where park superintendents have a fairly satisfactory tenure of office, and where they are allowed to manage, more or less, the development of park plans. There is an increasing tendency to employ competent landscape gardeners in the formation of parks, and other cheering signs combine to color our

FIG. 28. THE IDEAL PARK.
Rest, refreshment and inspiration in every feature. Prospect Park, Brooklyn.

hope for a steady improvement of park management along with the improvement of public taste.

When we consider the purposes of a public park as set forth above, we will see at once why the natural method of gardening best subserves them, and why they are the better fulfilled the more natural and pronouncedly rural the treatment is. Quietness, restfulness, simplicity, are the most desirable qualities. And this **emphasizes** the inappropriateness of pattern bedding, of loud color designs, and of all the tricks, intricacies, extravagancies and artificialities which eat up the gardener's time and the city's money, and which, by so much, render the park unfit for its best service. It is said, with considerable truth, by gardeners and others, that the public demand the artificial color patterns. Many people feel obliged to cater to this taste, even though they regard it as childish. But it should be said that the disproportionate notice which such objects attract in a public park is not a safe measure of the satisfaction they give. Many visitors are benefited by the fresh grass and the cooling shade who do not notice the lawn and the trees; while those who exclaim most loudly over the wonderful Chinese puzzles in coleus are not helped by them in the smallest degree. Such vociferous features of park ornamentation may be very fairly compared with the crying evil of advertising displays. When once begun, there is no excess to which either one may not be compelled to go.

Part IV.

The Gardener's Materials.

CHAPTER XVI

A SELECT LIST OF TREES.

> Many large trees, especially elms, about a house, are a sure indication of family distinction and worth. Any evidence of care bestowed on these trees receives the traveler's respect as for a nobler husbandry than the raising of corn and potatoes. —*Henry David Thoreau.*
>
> It will not do to be exclusive in our tastes about trees. There is hardly one of them which has not peculiar beauties in some fitting place for it. —*Oliver Wendell Holmes.*

In any save the smallest places the trees form the framework of the plantings. They are the first to be considered, and the first to be placed. And unless they are felicitously selected and happily placed and well grown the whole composition is apt to fall to pieces, since it lacks the necessary framework.

Moreover, trees are sometimes able to make a whole landscape by themselves. A forest is frequently beautiful. And if there are pleasant openings, with long perspectives, and views of wooded hills, or of craggy mountains, or of river, lake or sea, the landscape requires little else to make it satisfying to the most fastidious taste.

Then, too, a tree is a beautiful thing by itself. Each good tree has its own peculiar and sufficient beauties, and even the blasted and storm-torn tree may make a fascinating picture. In all large plantings there should be included a number of specimen trees, so placed as to show their individual good qualities, and so grown as to possess those good qualities in the greatest measure.

For all these reasons the selection of suitable trees becomes one of the landscape gardener's first and most important duties. Familiarity with trees and a sympathetic understanding of their manners and moods is the best basis on which to make this choice; but the following notes, which make no claim to completeness, may be of some service to those who have not made trees a special study.

Ash.—There are three or four native species of ash which may usually be collected from the woods or bought from the nurseries. All are good. They are excellent for large masses, and will bear comparatively thick planting.

Beech.—The common American beech is a fine tree where it will succeed. It is not practicable to mass it except in waste places, on hillsides, and the like. An occasional single tree in rich soil makes a specimen to be proud of. The Purple-leaved beech is a good tree of its color; but one or two will be enough for a very large place.

Birch.—Pyramidal and weeping birches have found many buyers during recent years. However, they partake more of the nature of curiosities than of indigenous trees, and are not to be recommended. Nearly all the native forms and species are good in their place, however, in garden planting, though any of them must be sparingly used. The White birch, Canoe birch and Yellow birch deserve special mention.

Butternut.—See Walnut.

Catalpa.—*Catalpa speciosa* is the species most planted. It makes a small or moderate sized tree, with large foliage, which is quite ornamental; and the species is further desirable for its fine display of flowers. *Catalpa bignonioides* and Tea's Japan Hybrid are good sorts less frequently planted.

Cedar.—The Red cedar, *Juniperus Virginiana*, is a fine ornamental evergreen much used in the western states, but scarcely known in some parts of the east. It is suitable for almost every situation where evergreens may be used; it can be massed with fine effect; it has a very attractive color; and other qualities recommend it for more general notice.

COFFEE TREE.—This beautiful ornamental tree, *Gymnocladus Canadensis*, makes a good specimen on almost any lawn. Not more than two or three are usually desirable, but they should not be omitted.

ELM.—The American elm is the typical American tree, and the one indispensable street tree. It is, perhaps, the most generally useful ornamental tree we have. No other elm is so good as the common species, though the following are well worth using for special purposes: Slippery elm, *Ulmus fulva*, English elm, *U. campestris*, Huntingdon elm, *U. Huntingdoni*, Wych elm, *U. Montana*.

GINGKO.—This strange tree, sometimes called the Maidenhair tree, makes an odd and pretty specimen, but is not suited to grouping. It makes a very good street tree when well grown.

HACKBERRY.—Sometimes called Nettle tree, *Celtis occidentalis*. This is a good, hardy tree, especially desirable in the western prairie states.

HONEY LOCUST.—This is one of our very best shade and ornamental trees. Its very large thorns, which sometimes prove annoying, may be avoided by securing thornless trees. These thornless trees may be found in almost any nursery.

HORSE-CHESTNUT.—This is a fine tree for small groups. It is not useful in masses, and not at its best in street planting. For grouping, the Ohio Buckeye or Western horse-chestnut is a good tree of small size.

KOELREUTERIA.—*Koelreuteria paniculata* has found many friends in this country, and may be seen in many parks and private places. It makes a small tree, fifteen to thirty feet high, with feathery pinnate leaves, and pretty yellow blossoms. To be chosen for middle-ground plantings, and used in small numbers.

LINDEN.—The American linden or Basswood is a good park tree, and also good for street planting. It deserves more general use.

MAGNOLIAS.—The magnolias seem most in keeping with southern landscapes, but many of them are useful as far north as New York city. Among the best species are *Magnolia conspicua*, *M. glauca*, *M. Soulangeana*, *M. macrophylla*, *M. stellata*, and *M. Lennei*.

MAPLES.—This is one of our noblest genera of trees. The common Sugar maple is a typical American tree and one of the most valuable for planting anywhere where it will thrive. In the western states it does not succeed, but is there replaced by the Silver or Soft maple, *Acer dasycarpum*. A fine, semi-weeping variety of this latter species is Wier's Cut-leaved maple, which is especially suitable for specimen planting in grounds of moderate extent. Schwerdler's maple is another fine ornamental variety. The Japanese maples are not hardy in the northern states. Though very satisfactory specimens are sometimes grown as far northward as Massachusetts, they are not generally successful beyond New York, and are at their best in the latitude of Washington. The Norway maple, *Acer platanoides*, makes a fine ornamental, street or shade tree. The Striped maple or moosewood, *Acer Pennsylvanicum*, is rather a large shrub than a tree, but is very fine for masses on sloping banks, for small screens, and similar purposes. The Mountain maple, *A. spicatum*, may be used in the same way.

MULBERRY.—The native American mulberry, *Morus rubra*, makes a good tree, and should be oftener chosen for general planting. The Russian mulberry and the Multicaulis mulberry are useful treated as shrubs. They may be worked into thickets and cut back from year to year.

A SELECT LIST OF TREES. 111

OAK.—Oaks are slow to grow, but they are worth waiting for. Almost every species is desirable for planting in parks and private grounds. Special mention may be given to the American White oak, *Quercus alba*, Swamp White oak, *Q. bicolor*, and the Scarlet oak, *Q. coccinea*. A dozen other extremely valuable species may be selected from almost any catalog.

PAULOWNIA.—This fine tree is seldom seen in perfection. Perhaps it is difficult to grow, though the experience of gardeners generally does not enforce this point. It does fairly well as far north as New York city, where some excellent specimens may be seen in Central Park. At Washington it is perhaps at its best.

PINE.—The genus Pinus contains the best of the evergreen trees, though for general park planting spruces are more easily managed. The best park pines are the Austrian, the Scotch, the White, *Pinus Strobus*, and the Dwarf Mugho. The latter makes a small, round-topped tree six to ten feet high, which is very attractive in certain situations.

PLUMS.—Pissard's plum is the one most commonly chosen for ornamental planting. This makes a clean, pretty, small tree, with bright, red foliage. It cannot be used in quantity. Several of the native plums, particularly *Prunus Americana*, are suitable for more frequent use in general composition.

POPLAR.—Several of the poplars are useful, particularly on account of their easy and rapid growth. They are, however, short-lived, and sometimes objectionable on account of their cottony seeds, which they sow broadcast. The Lombardy poplar has its own peculiar and obvious role in gardening practice.

SPRUCE.—Next to the pines, the spruces are our finest evergreens, and are, perhaps, even more useful than the former in general ornamental planting. The **best are the Norway,** White, Black and Colorado.

Sweet Gum.—This tree is especially suitable to the southern states, where, in artistic effect, it takes the place of the Sugar maple in the north. Where it succeeds well it may be planted in masses of almost any size.

Sycamore, Plane tree or Buttonwood.—The American sycamore is one of the very finest street trees we have, as one will readily believe after seeing it on the Capitol grounds at Washington. It is also useful in general park composition, the striking color and texture of its foliage marking it for special notice. It is not hardy north of Vermont, and not at its best north of Pennsylvania.

Thorn Trees.—The various species of the genus Cratægus make fine additions to lawn plantings, their effect being usually somewhat picturesque. Their small size adapts them to certain positions. Among the best native species may be named *Cratægus crus-galli, C. tomentosa,* and *C. coccinea.* The English hawthorn, *C. oxyacantha,* is sometimes planted in this country with fair success.

Tulip Tree, *Liriodendron Tulipifera.*—This is a good tree for situations where something large is required. It may be massed in any quantity. Prefers good soil.

Walnut.—The common Black walnut makes a fine tree, though it is slow of growth. The Japanese walnuts may sometimes be planted to advantage. The common butternut seldom makes a good tree, but it has characteristic foliage which makes it useful for planting with other trees.

Willow.—Many of the willows are useful, especially on low, moist land. The best are Royal willow, *Salix regalis,* the Shining willow, *S. lucida,* the Laurel-leaved willow, *S. laurifolia,* and the Golden willow, *S. vittelina aurea.* The Babylon willow is good in spite of its weeping habit. In general, weeping willows are to be avoided, unless an exception be made for cemeteries.

CHAPTER XVII.

THE BEST SHRUBS.

> Deciduous shrubs are, beyond all question, the most important element in planting small grounds.
> *C. S. Sargent.*
>
> If one-tenth the trouble wasted on carpet bedding and other fleeting, though costly, rubbish, had been spent on flowering shrubs, our gardens would be much the better for it. There are no plants so neglected as flowering shrubs.
> *Wm. Robinson.*
>
> The wild shrubs which skirt the waysides have a beauty beyond that of the cultivated exotics in spaded gardens.
> *Wilson Flagg.*

To some unfortunate persons masses and borders of loose growing shrubbery suggest nothing but neglected roadsides and pasture grounds. The commonness of such materials, and the ease with which unthoughtful persons may pass them by, seem to indicate a certain crudity, if not a real vulgarity, in the bushes and branches. But this feeling is founded upon an untrained sympathy,—upon a true lack of feeling for nature,—upon notions of ornamental planting which are in the highest degree incorrect. There is nothing so crude and vulgar in gardening as an over-display of colors (which are nearly always inharmonious among themselves). An appetite for these gaudy colors indicates an untrained taste, just as an appetite for dime novels indicates a poor taste in literature, or as a preference for noisy street songs indicates a lack of training in music. The more refined enjoyment and the most deeply pleasurable sensations aroused by any art are those which arise from delicate colorings, from subtle modulations, from almost imperceptible distinctions. And so the nature-lover delights in the most delicate tones and tints of grays and greens and browns, like those of the pussy willow and the roadside dogwood; and he revels in the beautiful variety of texture offered by the spirea, the sumach and the Judas tree.

We have already called attention to the usefulness of shrubs in naturalistic plantings, and need not repeat what has been said. But shrubs are also indispensable in all other systems of gardening, and a study of the species and varieties at command must be the first business of the gardener. The following list is not at all complete, but is meant to include the hardier and more useful kinds. There are enough for most plantings, for one must not make the mistake of trying to plant everything. A dozen well-selected species give a better effect than two hundred sorts huddled and crowded and jumbled together.

One frequently sees shrubs tied up in straw, or laid down and covered, or otherwise carefully protected for the winter. This has to be done with certain species in certain situations to keep them alive. But there are so many perfectly hardy shrubs, able to withstand everything that comes, that such labor may be entirely avoided. In fact, those plants which have to be coddled through bad weather and favored above their neighbors always give a suggestion of unnaturalness to the place. They seem to be exotic,—foreign to the situation. The perfectly wild garden, able to care for itself and always at home with its surroundings, has a certain permanency and unity of effect which no other garden can have.

Shrubs should be given proper pruning; but they should be spared the sort they often get. Only in very exceptional circumstances should the tops be sheared, or the growth cut back at the extremities. This spoils at once the graceful drooping habit which is separately characteristic of almost every species. When the pruning knife and the shears are to be applied to any shrub, they should usually cut out at the base. Old, straggling stems are cut away, and fresh, clean, vigorous sprouts come up in their places. Many species, like the sumachs, give the best results if they are cut back almost annually quite to the ground, and allowed to sprout afresh from the stools.

ALDER.—Several of the alders make very useful shrubs for border planting, particularly the European alder, which is rather a small tree if full grown. The Green or Mountain alder, *Alnus viridis*, is one of the best, three to eight feet tall. *Alnus incana* is a good plant of its size, eight to twenty feet.

AMALANCHIER CANADENSIS, Juneberry, Shad Bush.—The dwarf varieties, two to five feet high, are best for planting.

AMORPHA FRUTICOSA, False Indigo.—A good, hardy shrub. *Amorpha canescens*, Lead plant, is mostly herbaceous, with fine, soft, silvery foliage, and well worth more extensive planting. It has beautiful spikes of deep violet-purple flowers. One to three feet.

ARALIA SPINOSA, Hercules Club.—Bears immense leaves which give a striking, somewhat tropical effect. Six to eighteen feet.

BERBERIS, Barberry.—Very useful shrubs. The common species is from Europe, but is naturalized in many parts of the eastern states. The Purple-leaved barberry is a variety of this. *B. Thunbergii* is a small shrub from Japan with beautiful, delicate foliage, taking a fine red color after frost.

CALYCANTHUS FLORIDUS, Spice Bush.—A small shrub with very sweet scented flowers.

CARAGANA, Pea Tree.—*C. frutescens* is a low shrub, bearing an abundance of bright yellow, pea-like flowers in spring. *C. arborescens* is similar, but larger.

CEPHALANTHUS OCCIDENTALIS, Button Bush.—A hardy native shrub of wide distribution, making a round head; foliage good; flowers white, abundant, in globular heads in spring. Four to eight feet.

CERCIS CANADENSIS, Judas tree, Red bud.—A small tree with pretty bark and fine foliage; covered with red blossoms early in spring before the appearance of leaves.

CHIONANTHUS VIRGINICA, Fringe tree.—A large shrub or small tree, inclined to bear too little foliage, but having an abundance of white blossoms about lilac-flowering time.

CLETHRA ALNIFOLIA, White Alder.—A useful native shrub. Three to ten feet.

CORNUS, Dogwood. The dogwoods are among our best shrubs. No one should think of planting a place without them. The native red-branched species, *C. stolonifera* and *C. Baileyi*, are especially desirable. *C. paniculata* is also a native species, a good grower, and desirable for its flowers. *C. sericea*, *C. mas*, *C. sanguinea* and *C. florida* are all good.

CYDONIA JAPONICA (*Pyrus Japonica*), Japan quince.—Much cultivated in this country. Desirable chiefly on account of its brilliant scarlet flowers in early spring.

DAPHNE.—*D. mezereum* is a deciduous low shrub with rose-colored flowers; one to three feet. *D. cneorum* is a hardy, evergreen undershrub from Europe, and a great favorite with some planters.

DEUTZIA.—The deutzias are not quite hardy in the north, but can usually be depended on in the middle states, where they are very valuable. There are three useful species: *D. crenata*, *D. scabra* and *D. gracilis*.

DIERVILLA FLORIDA, Weigelia.—Included in this species are most of the shrubs sold as *Diervilla rosea*, *Weigelia alba*, etc. There are many varieties, mostly hardy, good growers and profuse bloomers. The foliage, however, is a trifle coarse.

ELDER.—The common American elder, *Sambucus Canadensis*, Fig. 29, is a shrub of no mean artistic capabilities. It is fine for massing against trees and along woodland borders, and for working into various compositions. The Golden elder is a pretty shrub for use in limited quantity.

ELEAGNUS, Oleaster.—*E. longipes* has been widely sold in recent years and is a good shrub, with ornamental and edible fruit. *E. argentea* is also planted, but is not so desirable.

EUONYMUS ATROPURPUREUS, Burning bush, or Strawberry tree.—Well known shrub with bright orna-

FIG. 29. THE AMERICAN ELDER.

mental fruit which persists long into the winter. Not hardy in the north.

EXOCHORDA GRANDIFLORA.—A fine shrub, bearing beautiful white blossoms in spring. Deserves more general planting.

FORSYTHIA, Golden-Bell.—One of the very finest shrubs for the latitude of New York and southward, especially *F. viridissima* and the commercial *F. Fortunei*, which bear great quantities of brilliant yellow flowers in early spring. These are quite commonly planted and form one of the most attractive features of the spring landscape in parts of New Jersey, Pennsylvania, Delaware, Maryland and Virginia. *Forsythia suspensa* of the catalogs is a weeping or semi-prostrate form.

HYDRANGEA PANICULATA GRANDIFLORA, The Hardy Hydrangea.—There are several forms of this, but the spreading shrub with large flowers is best. One of the best and most reliable hardy shrubs, giving a great

FIG. 30. HARDY HYDRANGEA PROPERLY PLANTED.

abundance of showy white flowers in autumn when blossoms are few. Four to eight feet.

HYPERICUM, St. John's Wort.—Small native shrubs of considerable usefulness, of which the best species are *H. Kalmianum, H. prolificum* and *H. aureum*.

KERRIA JAPONICA.—A pretty shrub with slender, delicate, bright green twigs, fresh green leaves and handsome yellow flowers. Well worth planting. Three to eight feet.

LIGUSTRUM, Privet.—One of the best shrubby hedge plants, but available also for **massing**. Hardy and thrifty and bears shearing. The species mostly grown are *L. vulgare* and *L. ovalifolium*.

LILAC (Botanically *Syringa*).—The lilacs are old and never-to-be-forgotten favorites. They are capable of much greater beauty than is usually realized. They should be kept cut back to a reasonable hight, the old wood thinned out, and a fresh, vigorous growth kept up by liberal manuring. The fine new varieties, with magnificent large single or double flowers in numerous extremely rich colors, offer a chance for many new experiences with these old favorites. Sometimes the finer varieties may be successfully grafted upon old, established plants which give inferior blossoms.

LONICERA TARTARICA, Bush Honeysuckle.—A very common and very useful shrub. A profuse bloomer. Very hardy. Four to eight feet.

MYRICA GALE, Sweet gale, and *Myrica asplenifolia*, Sweet Fern, are well known, small native shrubs which add very much to certain effects when judiciously set in small masses in the shrubbery border.

PHILADELPHUS, Syringa, Mock Orange. — These shrubs are most remarkable for their abundance of very fragrant white flowers in spring. Like lilacs, they need to be rigorously clipped out to prevent the accumulation of old, unsightly wood. The best plan is to cut all the stems back to the ground at three or four years old, or even at two years old if the growth of new wood justifies it. This keeps up a rotation of fresh, clean shoots. The best species are *P. grandiflorus*, *P. coronarius* and *P. Gordonianus*. Six to ten feet.

POTENTILLA FRUTICOSA, Cinquefoil.—A native shrub with bright yellow flowers. Hardy and inclined to be weedy in some sandy soils. Three to four feet.

PRUNUS, Plums and Cherries.—Nearly all the native plums and cherries are worth planting for ornamental purposes. The Beach plum, *Prunus maritima,* is one of the most useful, though for larger plants selected varieties of *P. Americana* make the finest of small trees. The Sand cherries, *P. pumila*, and *P. Besseyi*, growing from two to five feet high, are excellent; while for heavy masses in certain places the common Choke cherry is one of the best species known. It is vigorous, clean and healthy, though occasionally denuded by caterpillars.

Rhododendrons.—These magnificent ornamental plants are hardy in most situations and not usually difficult to grow. There are many wonderful and striking varieties offered by the nurserymen, but the beginner will hardly be able to discriminate their merits.

Rhus, Sumach.—The sumachs are mostly all very hardy and good ornamental plants. Their spreading, luxuriant pinnate foliage gives a peculiar and somewhat tropical suggestion. In most places they are best if the old growth is constantly cut out and the vigorous young shoots depended on. Their colors in autumn are especially desirable. *Rhus glabra* is probably best, followed by *R. copallina* and *R. typhina*. *R. Cotinus*, the Smoke tree, is quite different from the others. It is a well known shrub, five to ten feet high, bearing large feathery wands of reddish or purplish abortive blossoms.

Ribes Aureum.—A native currant, now often cultivated for fruit as well as for ornament. It bears many pretty, spicy, sweet scented, bright yellow flowers in spring, and always shows a clean, attractive foliage. Four to seven feet. Other species of currants and gooseberries are also useful in shrubbery masses.

Roses.—Hardy flowering roses are usually best planted in beds by themselves; but many of the native species are remarkably fine if grown in the border with the other shrubbery. *Rosa lucida*, *R. blanda* and nearly all the native species may be planted. The Sweet Brier and the Prairie rose, *R. setigera*, are among the best.

The Japanese rose, *R. rugosa,* is also a very fine shrub for general planting.

Rubus odoratus.—The flowering raspberry is one of the most useful and neglected of native shrubs. It should generally be used in small masses for the emphasis which its large, striking foliage gives. Three to five feet. Other brambles are very useful in many places.

Salix, Willow.—Most of the willows tend to be trees rather than shrubs, but many of them can be grown as shrubs if severely cut back. They are especially desirable for the delicate gray-greens which they give in spring, and some of them for the brightness of their twigs in winter. *Salix vitellina* of horticulturists has beautiful bright golden twigs. *S. lucida* is especially remarkable for its shining foliage. The so-called weeping willows grafted in the top of a straight trunk are to be avoided.

Spireas form, on the whole, the finest and most useful group of shrubs we have. Their hardiness, thrift, grace, floriferousness, all recommend them. Probably the best one is the horticulturist's *Spiræa Van Houttei,* sometimes called Bridal Wreath. No grounds anywhere ought to lack this. Then come *S. prunifolia* and *S. hypericifolia.* The former has specially beautiful foliage. The latter is much like a small edition of Van Houtt. *S. Thunbergii* is small (one to three feet) and very delicate and graceful in growth and in foliage, but not fully hardy northward. The golden spiræa (*S. aurea,* Hort.) is a fine, upright grower, with good, yellowish foliage, and bright stems in winter. Four to ten feet.

Symphoricarpus racemosus, Snowberry.—A good native shrub, with white berries in autumn. Two to five feet. *S. vulgaris,* Coral berry or Indian currant, is very common in the central and western states, and is well worth planting. It is graceful of growth and bears quantities of persistent bright red berries. Two to five feet.

VIBURNUM OPULUS, Snowball or Guelder rose.—This is a fine, strong-growing shrub giving abundant white blossoms. Other viburnums are also desirable, as *V. plicatum, V. lantanoides, V. tomentosum,* etc.

CHAPTER XVIII.

HARDY PERENNIALS.

> Die Zahl der Freunde von Stauden oder perennierenden Gewaechsen hat in den letzten Jahren ganz bedeutend zugenommen; man darf nur bei einem Ausflug die Gaerten und Gaertchen der Blumenfreunde, in der Stadt, wie auf dem Lande, aufmerksam betrachten, da wird man beobachten koennen, dass Stauden schon viel Verwendung gefunden haben und hoffentlich noch mehr finden werden.
> *J. Biemueller.*

The hardy herbaceous perennials, as a class, are the easiest to manage, the cheapest and the most naturalistic in the effect they give, of all the plants that grow. When once planted they need very little further care. Many of them need none at all, and will thrive and multiply for years in the grass or among the shrubs without the slightest attention. Growing thus at full freedom they give a wild, woodsy air to a place which nothing else can furnish quite so well. Their ability to take care of themselves year after year makes them very cheap. There has been a very healthy and gratifying tendency in recent years toward the more general use of such material, but there is no likelihood that it will soon be overdone.

Hardy perennials may be used in almost any situation where plants are wanted at all. They may grow under the trees, among the shrubs, in rockeries, along the borders of ponds and rivulets, on sloping banks, in borders by themselves, in shade or sun; in fact, it is very hard to go amiss with them unless, indeed, they are put into flower beds. It is a very convenient way to outline a border with herbaceous perennials, among which and in front of which the annuals are planted from year to year. One of the best ways is to mix them with the shrubbery, usually, of course, bringing them somewhat in front of the larger woody shrubs, as shown in Fig. 31. Many of them are excellent simply scattered thickly in the grass. Here they become naturalized and lead their own careless-thrifty lives. Buttercups and daisies live in that way. Columbines and golden-rods give great satisfaction when similarly grown. So do anemones, trilliums, asters, claytonias, erigerons, pent-

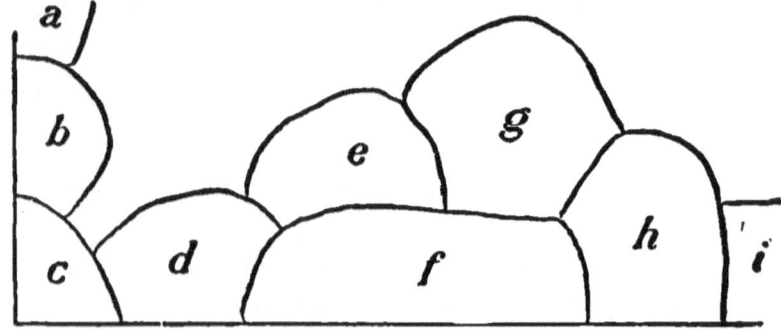

FIG. 31. SUGGESTION FOR BORDER PLANTING.

For planting with perennials: *a*, *Papaver nudicaule*, Iceland poppy. *b*, *Pentstemon acuminatus*. *c*, Phlox hybrids. *d*, *Aster Novæ-Angliæ*. *e*, *Aquilegia chrysantha*, columbine. *f*, Hollyhocks. *g*, *Coreopsis grandiflora*. *h*, *Chrysanthemum maximum*. *i*, Peonies, or *Œnothera Fraseri*.

For planting with annuals: *a*, Nasturtiums, dwarf. *b*, Shirley poppies. *c*, *Gaillardia Lorenziana*. *d*, Branching asters. *e*, *Antirrhinum*, snapdragon. *f*, Sunflower, "Stella." *g*, *Coreopsis Drummondii*, "Golden Wave." *h*, Petunias. *i*, *Phlox Drummondii*.

For mixed planting: *a*, Nasturtiums. *b*, Shirley poppies. *c*, Gladioli. *d*, Branching asters. *e*, *Aquilegia chrysantha*, columbine. *f*, *Helianthus orgyalis*, willow-leaved sunflower. *g*, Calendula, or Large Marigolds. *h*, *Digitalis gloxiniæflora*, foxglove. *i*, *Lilium speciosum rubrum*.

stemons, and many others. Of course, the most of these cannot be grown in a lawn which is kept mowed; but there should be some unmowed lawn on any place which has the room.

Many of the hardy perennials can be grown easily from seed. Usually it is best to sow the seed in a specially prepared bed or cold frame, from which the seedlings are transplanted to pots, nursery rows, **or** directly to their permanent places. Many of them are propagated more easily by division. Or the ready-grown plants may be bought directly from the nurseryman; and as each investment in such plants is a permanent one, the expense is comparatively small.

It would be entirely impossible, within the limits of this work, to enumerate and describe the most of the good herbaceous perennials. The following list is offered merely as a suggestion to those who are very much unacquainted with such plants. The author has endeavored to select those easiest to grow and of widest usefulness; but as such a selection is a very personal matter anyone else who is acquainted with herbaceous perennials will be likely to choose a somewhat different list.

Aconitum, Monkshood. — A charming group of plants, though some are poisonous. The best are *A. napellus*, *A. autumnale* and *A. uncinatum*.

Anemone, Wind Flower. — In many species and varieties, all good. Mostly flowering early; usually white, sometimes blue. Among the best are *A. sylvestris*, *A. nemorosa*, *A. Pennsylvanica*, *A. patens Nuttalliana*, *A. Japonica*, and many horticultural varieties, both double and single.

Aquilegia, Columbine. — One of the most valuable groups of hardy plants. Easy to grow from seed. The best species are *A. Canadensis*, *A. cærulea*, *A. vulgaris* and *A. chrysantha*, though there are many other fine ones.

Asclepias contains several good plants, of which *A. tuberosa* is best. It grows in tufts, twelve to eighteen inches high, with large heads of orange blossoms in midsummer.

Aster. — Several of the asters are hardy perennials, and many are very ornamental. The following deserve special mention: *A. lævis*, *A. Novæ-Angliæ*, *A. Novi-Belgii*, *A. cordifolius*, *A. alpinus*, *A. ericoides*.

BOCCONIA CORDATA (*B. Japonica*).—A large, strong-growing plant, with large leaves. Fine for emphasis at medium distances. Five to eight feet.

CALLIRHOE INVOLUCRATA.—A good, small, trailing plant with an abundance of purplish flowers.

CAMPANULA, Bluebell, Harebell.—Easy to grow and always attractive. The genus numbers several fine species, such as *C. Carpathica, C. medium, C. nobilis, C. punctata, C. rotundifolia, C. grandis,* etc.

CHRYSANTHEMUM.—This genus contains several hardy species, some of them known as daisies or marguerites. Probably *C. maximum* is the best, though others are very good.

COREOPSIS.—Fine, free-flowering plants with large, golden blossoms. *C. grandiflora* and *C. lanceolata* are the best of the perennial species. Fine for cut flowers.

DELPHINIUM, Larkspur.—The perennial larkspurs are very showy and valuable plants. They may be had in numerous species and varieties. Those commonly grown are hybrids.

DIGITALIS, Foxglove.—Well known plants of easiest culture, free flowering and always desirable. The commonest species, with very large flowers in a variety of colors, goes under the doubtful name of *D. gloxiniæflora;* but *D. lanata, D. Siberica* and *D. grandiflora* are equally fine.

HELENIUM.—A very fine and striking plant, particularly the variety, *H. autumnale superbum.* Furnishes a dazzling glow of yellow late in summer when flowers are scarce. Six to eight feet.

HELIANTHUS, Sunflower.—Some of the perennial species are very useful in border composition. The best are *H. Maximillani* and *H. orgyalis.* These give very striking, though easy and natural, effects.

HOLLYHOCK.—The old favorite, and one of the most artistically effective plants known. In many colors, single and double. Subject to severe attacks of **rust**, which sometimes kill the plants. In such cases burn the old plants and all the litter around them and plant anew in a different spot.

FIG. 32. ICELAND POPPY.

LEPACHYS.—A very desirable genus comprising only a few species, of which *L. pinnata* and *L. columnaris* are worth first trial.

ŒNOTHERA.—Comprises several good species, mostly with large yellow flowers. The best are *Œ. Missouriensis*, *Œ. fruticosa major* and *Œ. Fraseri*.

PAPAVER, Poppy.—One of the most delicate and beautiful of hardy plants is the Iceland poppy, *Papaver nudicaule*. The Royal scarlet poppy, *P. orientale*, is a large and very showy species.

PENTSTEMON.—This genus numbers several of the very best herbaceous plants known to horticulture. They are hardy and easy to manage. Among the best are *P. digitalis*, *P. grandiflorus*, *P. pubescens*, *P. confertus*, *P. barbatus Torreyi*, *P. acuminatus* and *P. ovatus*. There are several others, and not a poor one among them.

PEONY.—Too well known to need remark. Usually grown alone on the lawn, but much finer when massed in the border against the shrubbery. Propagate by division.

PHLOX.—The well-known and showy perennial phlox of the gardens is *P. paniculata*, often called *P. decussata*, which has numberless fine varieties. Several of the native species are also very useful for border planting, especially *P. maculata* and *P. divaricata*.

RUDBECKIA, Coneflower.—Large, strong-growing, hardy plants. The best is the new variety, Golden Glow, which belongs to the species *R. laciniata*. *R. maxima*, *R. hirta* and *R. Newmanii* are excellent.

SOLIDAGO, Goldenrod.—A characteristically American genus of incomparable beauty. The only reason people do not plant them extensively is that they grow wild so abundantly. But no garden should be without its masses of goldenrod. The best species for planting are *S. Canadensis*, *S. sempervirens*, *S. juncea*, *S. nemoralis* and *S. speciosa*.

SPIRÆA.—Several of the spiræas are herbaceous. They are all useful. The best known are *S. aruncus*, *S. astilboides*, *S. palmata* and *S. venusta*.

TRILLIUM.—One of the most beautiful blossoms of early spring. *T. grandiflorum*, bearing large, pure white flowers, is best. Prefers a somewhat shady place.

CHAPTER XIX.

THE INDISPENSABLE ANNUALS.

> The greatest possibilities with color in the garden depend upon the annuals. —*F. Schuyler Mathews.*
>
> For the best and most continuous display of flowers during the whole summer season, annual plants are essential. —*E. O. Orpet.*

The old-fashioned flower gardens were largely made up of annuals. Among flowers, by far the larger part of the old-time favorites were annuals; and it is probable that nine out of ten persons to-day, if asked to mention their favorite flowers (florists' stock excepted), would name annuals. Sweet peas, pansies, asters, cosmos, nasturtiums,—these have a hold on people which they will never lose.

And so, while it is possible to find many pleasant gardens,—in snug back yards, or window boxes or tomato cans,—without trees and shrubs and perennials, the annuals are omnipresent. Their great variety, their adaptability to all needs and circumstances, the innumerable, characteristically beautiful ways they have of expressing themselves, make them always indispensable. A striking effect produced by annuals is seen in Fig. 33.

Almost all of the annuals may be grown successfully by sowing the seeds where the plants are to stand. This is done when the weather is warm enough in spring, and as soon as the soil is in good workable condition. The seed bed should always be thoroughly prepared, with good drainage and an abundance of well-decomposed fertilizer worked in. But it is much the best plan, especially in northern latitudes, wherever it

130 LANDSCAPE GARDENING.

FIG. 33. ANNUALS IN BACK YARD GARDEN.
Cosmos, Castor Bean and Morning Glories.

can be done, to start the plants in hotbeds, cold frames,* greenhouses, or boxes of earth in the house, from which they are transplanted to the open ground. Considerable time is gained in this way,—often one or two months. Nearly all the annual species may be handled in this way. There are a few exceptions. But many sorts make much better plants by transplanting; and it is often advisable to transplant the seedlings once before they reach their final stations in the grounds.

The commonest error, in growing annuals, is to plant them in flower beds. This mistake is frequently made with other plants, but never so persistently and disastrously as with phloxes, zinnias, marigolds and their like. If a strictly geometrical scheme is intended, or if the garden is one of the old Italian style, with a high wall about it, then flower beds will fit the place. But in the free and natural door-yard gardening, with which we are most concerned, the whole picture is sadly disfigured when it is cut full of holes to receive strange, detached bunches of unwilling flowers in varied assortment. There they stand about uncomfortably through the summer, each bunch of flowers jealous of its neighbors, all appearing to be afraid of overstepping the circumscribing bricks, stones or oyster shells which hem them in, all chafing at the restraint, and all wishing they were safely away in the woods, where they might clamber down the banks or revel in the grass the way flowers were meant to do.

The annual plants ought to be put, not into beds, but into the borders with the perennials and the shrubs. Or if shrubs and perennials are not grown, then the annuals have the border to themselves. Arranged in

---

*Directions for making cold frames and hotbeds of all sorts may be found in any general work on gardening. See Bailey's Garden-Making, Taft's Greenhouse Construction, Henderson's Gardening for Profit, etc., etc.

this way, they are capable of some of the most brilliant and satisfying effects which plants can ever give. In the irregularity and informality of the border it makes no difference if one plant or a whole lot of plants fails to grow. The irregularity is not destroyed! Or if some celandines or dandelions crowd into a half occupied nook somewhere, there is no harm done, for flowers are what we want. It would be different if we wanted flower beds.

The first and easiest and greatest improvement to be made in hundreds of front yards would be to obliterate the flower beds entirely,—sod them over, and leave an open greensward where they have stood in the middle of the lawn,—and move the flowers into the side borders.

It is hardly necessary to describe the principal annuals nor to give directions for their cultivation; but the following partial list, with scattering notes, is appended merely as a suggestion of the manifold riches at command.

Asters.—The annual or "China" asters have been very much improved in recent years. The old-time asters were too stiff and formal to gain much sympathy, but the new sorts, particularly the branching and the chrysanthemum flowering sections, are free and graceful and very fine. The new Japanese asters are also informal and agreeable. The better strains of the German quilled asters are extremely good, and quite different from other varieties. Asters should always be started in a hotbed and transplanted if possible.

Alyssum.—A good old favorite. Works nicely into the edges of the flower border.

Ageratum.—Constant bloomer during summer, in white and bright blue; good in the edges of borders. Six to eighteen inches high.

Antirrhinum, Snapdragon.—Many fine colors, from white nearly to black, in dwarf and standard varieties.

To be used mostly in small masses. Six inches to two feet.

BALSAMS.—Old-time favorites, but not very useful in composition with other plants. They do not transplant well.

CALENDULA, called Pot Marigold by some.—Thrifty and a constant bloomer, mostly in yellow and orange shades. Ten to eighteen inches.

CANDYTUFT.—Good, free flowering, hardy border plant, in several colors, pure white being best.

CENTAUREA, Corn Bottle, Blue Bottle, or Bachelor's Button.—Another old favorite, running mostly to light blues. A new strain of Marguerite centaureas has a better form and more substance to the blossoms.

CELOSIA, including Cockscomb. This group numbers some very ornamental plants, especially the feathered varieties and those with ornamental foliage.

COREOPSIS, Calliopsis.—All bright yellows, with unimportant exceptions. Some of the finest flowering plants grown for border or for cut flowers. *C. Drummondii* (var. Golden Wave) is best of the annual species. *C. tinctoria* gives many pretty dwarf varieties, and some with quilled, others with dark maroon, blossoms. One to three feet.

COSMOS.—One of the finest annuals, especially southward. Does not succeed well at the north. In white and several shades of pink and red. The white blossoms are prettiest. Three to six feet.

DATURA, Horn of Plenty, "Jimpson Weed."--A large, coarse plant, giving a striking effect at a little distance. Has conspicuous, large white flowers. Four to eight feet.

DIANTHUS, Pink.—A good old favorite, and worth more general cultivation at the present time. Many colors, single and double.

GAILLARDIA.—Fine flowers for border and for cutting; reds and yellows; somewhat daisy-like **in form,** except the double *G. Lorenziana*. Worth more extensive cultivation.

Nasturtium, Tropœolum.—One of the richest and finest annual plants in cultivation and deservedly popular. All varieties may be grown in the border, though the dwarfs are best. The tall sorts are extremely well adapted to window boxes, lawn vases, and to situations where they may fall over rocks or down short slopes. The new hybrids of Madame Gunter show many beautiful colors.

Pansy.—Known and admired of all. For small plantings buy plants of the florist in spring. To grow the plants sow the seed in the fall in cold frames, which are covered at the beginning of winter. Transplant from these early in spring. Or sow the seeds as early as possible in spring in the hotbed or in pots or boxes in the house. Buy good seed.

Petunia.—Very fine for heavy masses in the flower border. A solid block of petunias thirty or forty feet across gives a very striking effect, if not out of harmony with its surroundings. The free and easy luxuriance of growth and profusion of bloom cannot be surpassed by anything in the garden. Extra choice varieties may easily be grown from cuttings; but main dependence may be placed on seedlings grown in fall, winter or early spring, and transplanted to the open ground after all danger of frost is past.

Phlox.—The annual *Phlox Drummondii* is one of the finest border plants. Many people have become indifferent to it from having seen it so often grown in stiff, awkward flower beds. Such treatment takes all the grace and freedom out of the plant, which is inclined by nature to be a trifle stiff and serious. But when it is allowed to form free, irregular masses in the border, properly supported by other flowers, it is a very charming plant.

Poppy.—The annual poppies are very striking in color and graceful in form. They always seem at home in the mixed border, harmonizing with almost anything. The Shirley poppies are especially desirable, but there is hardly a variety grown which is not an acquisition.

Ricinus, Castor-oil bean.—These plants, of several different species, give grand summer effects. The varieties with dark foliage are especially beautiful. Should be started early.

Stocks.—Old favorites, but neglected in late years. Very useful in the border.

Sunflowers.—Several sorts, all useful on account of the emphasis they give to certain points in the border planting. Plant early.

Sweet Pea.—One of the finest plants known for cut flowers and quite indispensable, but not well adapted to the hardy border. They are usually best put by themselves, where they may have a trellis and good cultivation. They should be sown in the open ground at the earliest possible moment in the spring, or may even be sown in the fall. The selection of varieties is wholly a matter of personal taste. There are several useful little manuals which the sweet pea lover should consult.

Verbena.—The low, prostrate habit of verbenas does not best suit them to mixed plantings in the natural method. A few of them may be used, however, in certain parts of the border, especially where the plantings come directly beside a footpath.

Zinnias.—Well-known, old-fashioned flowers, but useful in many places. The newer varieties show some fine shades of color.

CHAPTER XX.

A FEW BULBOUS PLANTS.

> No garden should be without a bed of bulbs. Beginning so early in the season,—weeks and weeks before the blooming period of the earliest annuals,—their brilliant and beautiful flowers are enjoyed more than those of summer.
> *E. E. Rexford.*
>
> Nothing can exceed the brilliancy and variety of color displayed by their flowers, and nothing can be more simple than their culture. *Mrs. Loudon.*

Along with the herbaceous perennials naturally come the hardy and half-hardy bulbous plants. They have in general the same requirements and the same capabilities as the herbaceous perennials. Many of them will live untended in the open border quite without protection, and thrive and blossom year after year. Some require winter protection, but all of those named here will last without replanting for several or many years.

It is to be noted that few or none of these plants are desirable for their foliage. They are all grown for the brilliancy of their blossoms. This requires that they be judiciously set to show against shrubs or such other foliage-covered plants as shall give them a suitable background. This is seldom taken into consideration. Lilies, gladioli and irises are almost always planted by themselves. They are left without support. They look lost and out of place. Anyone can see, as soon as it is mentioned, how much better they would look comfortably grouped with other plants.

The following list includes the best bulbous plants, with a few which do not grow from the bulbs, but which, in view of the use we make of them, may be best understood just here.

CROCUSES.—Almost the first flowers of spring, and always welcome for their earliness and freshness. Where shrubs and herbaceous plants are grown in an open border, crocuses may be thickly planted in narrow rows along the extreme edge next the grass. One of the most satisfactory ways to grow crocuses is to scatter them thickly in the grass, where they will usually come up every spring without further care.

DAHLIA.—The dahlia is enjoying just now a well-deserved renewal of public favor. Many fine new varieties are being offered by the dealers, and great satisfaction is to be got out of their culture. The cactus varieties are the most informal and appeal more strongly than the older types to most tastes; but the single varieties and the smaller pompons, as well as the mammoth blossoms of the most regular outlines, have all their various agreeable expressions.

ERYTHRONIUM, Dog's-Tooth violet.—These little early flowering plants are very delicate and beautiful. There are several fine species and varieties, nearly all of which are hardy.

GLADIOLUS.—The gladiolus is one of the most striking and effective flowers in the garden when nicely grouped with other plants. When put by itself and with no company but an unpainted stick, it is one of the most awkward and ungainly sights on the lawn. The gladioli are especially useful for grouping in small masses among shrubs. There are hundreds of fine varieties, in many colors, but yellows and reds are best, especially reds. The bright reds and carmines seem to be the best suited to the character of the plants.

IRIS.—There are some fine, hardy, native irises, and a great many hardy and tender species of great beauty from all over the world which may be grown with a little care. Among the best are *I. Susiana* and *I. Siberica*. The many varieties of German iris are all desirable;

and the Japan irises, *I. Kœmpferi*, are among the most gorgeous flowers ever seen in temperate climates.

LILY.—The noblest of flowering plants. Lilies should be scattered liberally in every flower border. They harmonize well with shrubs and herbaceous perennials, and the annuals may be mixed with them to great advantage. The following are a few of the best species for garden culture: *L. auratum*, Gold-banded Japan lily, one of the most popular and magnificent; flowers

FIG. 34. LILIUM SPECIOSUM.

very large, white, banded with gold and spotted with red; requires replanting from time to time. *L. bulbiferum*, a moderate sized European species; flowers red. *L. Browni*, one of the finest, bears three to four flowers, seven to eight inches long, chocolate brown outside, pure white within. *L. Canadense*, the common meadow lily, hardy, abundant bloomer, useful, in several shades of red and yellow. *L. elegans*, a very showy species, with large flowers in several shades of red and orange.

A FEW BULBOUS PLANTS.

L. elegans fulgens (*Batemanniæ*) is especially showy and fine. *L. Grayi*, a fine, delicate, native species, small flowers, red. *L. puberulum* (*Humboldti*), very strong and handsome, bears large orange-red flowers. *L. Henryi*, a new and rare species, but one of the most magnificent; should be planted by everyone who can afford it; flowers large, orange. *L. Japonicum Krameri*, large flowers of a very delicate pink tint, quite unique. *L. longiflorum*, a fine, large, white lily. *L. candidum*, the common white lily, nearly hardy, a free bloomer and very attractive. *L. pardalinum*, flowers orange, with lighter center, a good sort. *L. superbum*, a strong native species, bearing large numbers of red or orange blossoms. *L. speciosum*, Fig. 34, one of the very best, especially the variety *rubrum*. *L. tenuifolium*, the Coral lily; somewhat dwarf, with many brilliant, coral-red blossoms; very desirable. *L. tigrinum*, the well-known tiger lily; good. Most of these are better if covered in winter with a mulch.

NARCISSUS.—This genus includes several plants of great usefulness in the hardy garden. The trumpet narcissi, often called daffodils, are especially fine, either in the general border or naturalized in the grass. Some of the best sorts for outdoor culture are Horsfieldi, Emperor, Empress, Bulbocodium, Poet narcissus, Trumpet Major and Incomparabilis. Narcissi can best be transplanted in June and July.

TUBEROSES may be planted in the flower garden or border with considerable satisfaction. They should be set in fall and covered with a mulch.

TULIPS make fine displays in early spring, and for a week the open bed in mid-lawn is almost bearable, so that we forget the manure heap which has been there all winter and the inharmoniousness of the plan in general. But tulips may also be scattered in the border with other plants, or even set into the turf. There are many magnificent species and varieties listed and described in all catalogs.

YUCCA.—Nurserymen usually classify the yuccas with the bulbous plants, and perhaps they are as much at home here as anywhere. They must be used with

FIG. 35. YUCCA FILAMENTOSA.
Central Park, New York.

caution, but in surroundings somewhat picturesque they may be introduced with fine effect. *Yucca filamentosa,* Fig. 35, is the species most generally used, but *Y. angustifolia* is also desirable.

CHAPTER XXI.

CLIMBERS.

> **I love these immense wreaths of vine which extend far and wide in rich green garlands, and which become, in autumn, of a splendid purple. . . . At the extremity of my garden the vine extends in long porticoes, through the arcades of which may be seen trees of all sorts and foliage of all colors.** *Alphonse Karr.*
>
> **As found growing wild, the hard-wooded climbers and trailers afford some of the most delightful bits of natural scenery to be met with. Many of these serve valuable purposes for embellishments in ornamental gardening.**
> *E. A. Long.*

In making up a landscape picture proper, climbers are of minor importance. Their chief use, in purely naturalistic compositions, is not for climbing, but for trailing over rocks, or down sloping banks, or for clambering over low bushes. In such situations as these they are very effective.

But when buildings are introduced, and fences have to be dealt with, and other more unsightly objects need amelioration or concealment, the climbers are indispensable. In the shading and adornment of porches they play no insignificant part in the list of the gardener's materials.

I wish to emphasize the fact that no climber ought to be planted on level ground unless there be first some suitable support on which it is to climb. It is not uncommon to find cases in which the climber was first planted, and afterward some crazy and impertinent structure was arranged to meet its demands. This is one of the ways of losing naturalness, along with all other kinds of beauty.

Wherever a permanent planting can be made, **perennial** climbing plants will usually be the more desirable. But for temporary and immediate effects, or to reinforce perennial climbers where they are too thin, or for window boxes, and similar purposes, the annual climbing plants are of great value. Some species of the latter may be started early in the house, and transplanted out of doors as soon as frost is past, so as to gain an earlier effect. The following brief list includes the most useful sorts.

HARDY PERENNIAL CLIMBERS.

ACTINIDIA.—White flowers with purple centers. Still rare in this country, but destined to be popular.

AKEBIA QUINATA.—A dainty little climber from Japan, with small, five-parted leaves. Desirable where a large quantity of foliage is not required.

AMPELOPSIS.—The American ivy, Virginia Creeper, or Woodbine, *A. quinquefolia*, is one of the commonest, best and most widely useful of all climbers. The Japanese, or Boston ivy, *A. Veitchii*, is excellent for covering stone or brick walls, particularly the latter.

ARISTOLOCHIA SIPHO, Dutchman's Pipe Vine.—A very hardy, vigorous climber, with large leaves. One of the best, especially in the northern states.

CELASTRUS SCANDENS, Bittersweet.—One of the very best and hardiest climbers. To be recommended everywhere.

CLEMATIS, Virgin's Bower.—Several species and horticultural varieties of this group come up for consideration wherever climbers are wanted. The thrifty species with garlands of white flowers,—*C. paniculata, C. flammula, C. Virginiana, C. montana,*—are the most useful. *C. Jackmanii* is always a favorite, for its large blue flowers, though it has nothing else to recommend it. Many other varieties bearing beautiful, showy flowers are to be had of the dealers.

LONICERA, Honeysuckle.—Hall's honeysuckle, with its white or yellowish, very fragrant flowers is a favorite plant, especially southward. The old-fashioned climbing Trumpet honeysuckle, *L. sempervirens*, is very useful for neglected situations.

MENISPERMUM CANADENSE, Moon Seed.—A slender, twining plant which makes a nice addition to a collection.

TECOMA, Trumpet Flower, or Trumpet Creeper.— This is a most excellent plant where a somewhat wayward informality of habit is agreeable to the surroundings. Deserves more general use.

WISTARIA.—An old-time favorite. Useful in many situations, but not sufficiently fresh and tidy in foliage to come under constant close observation.

ANNUAL CLIMBERS.

BALLOON VINE.—An old-time favorite, to be found in all the old-fashioned gardens. The puffy, inflated seed vessels which appear throughout the summer are the most striking feature.

ECHINOCYSTIS LOBATA, Climbing Cucumber. — A rapid-growing, luxuriant climber from the American woods, covered with garlands of white flowers throughout the season. One of the best for common planting.

HOP VINE.—One of the most rapid growing and useful climbers. It is one of the best annual plants for covering verandas or other large areas. The "Variegated-leaved Japan hop" is preferred by some, though the effect is not always good.

MAURANDYA.—Rather short climbers with abundant white, pink or violet-purple blossoms. Suited to more general use.

MINA.—A pretty and useful plant of the morning glory family, but with small flowers and lobed leaves.

Momordica, Balsam Apple.—A favorite in old-fashioned gardens, and always good.

Morning Glory, *Ipomœa*.—This glorious and old-fashioned climber has been too much neglected by modern amateur and professional gardeners. There are many magnificent new varieties now on the market, and they are so useful for many purposes that they ought to enjoy a new lease of public favor.

Sweet Pea.—The sweet pea needs no introduction or praise. In climbing over fences and low trellises it is thoroughly at home, while no known plant gives a finer harvest of flowers suitable for cutting.

Tropæolum, Nasturtium.—The climbing nasturtiums are extra fine for window boxes, lawn vases, and many other places. It is worth while, in planting nasturtiums, to choose the best-bred named varieties. The varieties known as "Lobb's nasturtiums" and the "Madame Gunter hybrids" are especially thrifty in growth and rich in gorgeous colors.

APPENDIX.

SOME BOOKS ON LANDSCAPE GARDENING.

The literature of landscape gardening is not extensive, but choice. Probably the best things, from the literary standpoint, connected with agriculture, horticulture and rural affairs, are by all odds the books and essays which deal with picture gardening. With this literature the earnest student or ambitious practical gardener will naturally wish to acquaint himself. For this reason there are here given a few references to the most useful and accessible works on the subject. The list is not at all full. Those who care for an extended bibliography of the subject may consult Mrs. Van Rensselaer's admirable book, "Art out of Doors," and also Mr. Henry Sargent Codman's notes in Vol. III (1890) of *Garden and Forest.*

Many of the best short essays on landscape gardening subjects are to be found in the volumes of our American horticultural journals. The old volumes of Downing's *Horticulturist,* of *Garden and Forest, American Gardening* and *Popular Gardening* are especially rich in matter of this sort. The classical essays of Andrew Jackson Downing, afterward collected and edited by George William Curtis for the volume of Rural Essays, appeared first as editorials in the *Horticulturist;* and the editorials of Professor Sargent and Mr. Stiles in *Garden and Forest* have, many of them, an equal permanent literary and technical value. The man or woman who is interested in following out the literature of gardening must not forget to give patient **study to** the files of these magazines.

For the student or reader who is thoroughly enthused with the spirit of landscape study, and especially if one is studying the subject for the sake of his own personal pleasure in it rather than for the immediate good he may derive in planting shrubs, there is another considerable field of literature which he will do well to explore to the full extent of his opportunities. These are the essays and books which, under one name and another, deal with the beauties of rural life and are filled with the atmosphere of woods, lakes and mountains. Merely as examples of such we may remember John Burroughs (of whose books Winter Sunshine should be named first in this connection), the essays of Donald G. Mitchell (Ik. Marvel), the diaries of Thoreau, and Charles Dudley Warner's Summer in a Garden. It would have been a pleasure to the writer to include a bibliography of these books in this chapter; but as that cannot be done, the reader will depend on librarians and book dealers who everywhere know and prize these books.

In the following much abridged list of books on landscape gardening only those are included which are of the most direct value to the beginner. By the time he has thoroughly studied these his horizon will have been so far enlarged that he can select his reading for himself better than anyone can do it for him.

EUROPEAN BOOKS.

AMHERST, ALICIA, History of Gardening in England, London, 1885. A very complete and satisfying treatise on the subject.

ANDRÉ, EDOUARD, L'Art des Jardins, 1879. The most complete and thoroughly useful work on this subject in any language. Finely illustrated.

BACON, LORD FRANCIS, Of Gardens, in his essays, 1625.

GILPIN, WILLIAM, Observations on Picturesque Beauty, 1786. Also, Remarks on Forest Scenery. The latter especially is worth careful reading.

JAEGER, H., Lehrbuch der Gartenkunst, 1877. One of the best German works on the subject. Probably the best history of landscape gardening in general is by the same author, and is entitled Gartenkunst und Gaerten, Sonst und Jetzt. 1885.

LOUDON, J. C., Hints on the Formation of Gardens and Pleasure Grounds, 1812.

PRICE, SIR UVEDALE, An Essay on the Picturesque as Compared with the Sublime and the Beautiful, and on the Use of Studying Pictures for the Purpose of Improving Real Landscape, 1794. This is published in many editions. The best one (*fide* Mrs. Van Rensselaer) is that of 1842, edited by Sir Thomas Dick Lauder.

REPTON, HUMPHREY, Observations on the Theory and Practice of Landscape Gardening, 1793. This is the most valuable of early works on the practice of landscape gardening. Its instructions are still of great value.

ROBINSON, WILLIAM, The English Flower Garden, 1883. There are several editions of this magnificent work. The later ones have been revised by the author, and a great deal of descriptive and illustrative matter added. Describes and illustrates large numbers of plants. A valuable book of reference. The same author has written The Parks, Promenades and Gardens of Paris, 1869. An interesting and suggestive volume.

SHENSTONE, WILLIAM, Unconnected Thoughts on Gardening, 1764.

WHEATLEY, THOMAS, Observations on Modern Gardening, 1770. In various editions, the first edition being published anonymously. This is one of the best early works on the theory of landscape gardening.

AMERICAN BOOKS.

BAILEY, L. H., Garden-Making, New York, 1898. Contains some useful chapters on landscape gardening.

DOWNING, A. J., A Treatise on the Theory and Practice of Landscape Gardening, adapted to North America, 1841. This was the first great work on landscape gardening in America, and one which will always remain a classic. There are many editions.

HOWE, WALTER, The Garden, as Considered in Literature by Certain Polite Writers. New York, 1890. Contains selections from Pliny the Elder, Pliny the Younger, Lord Bacon, Sir William Temple, Joseph Addison, Alexander Pope, Lady Montague, Thomas Wheatley, Oliver Goldsmith, Horace Walpole and John Evelyn. A dainty and companionable little book.

LONG, E. A., Ornamental Gardening for Americans, New York, 1885. An excellent treatise, covering especially the details of practice.

MAYNARD, S. T., Landscape Gardening as Applied to Home Decorations. Illustrated, New York, 1899.

PARSONS, SAMUEL, JR., Landscape Gardening, 1891. A beautiful book, containing much practical information.

PARSONS, S., JR., How to Plant the Home Grounds. Illustrated, New York, 1899.

PLATT, CHARLES A., Italian Gardens, New York, 1894. Nicely illustrated. The best monograph we have of the Italian style in Italy.

ROSE, N. JONSSON, Lawns and Gardens. Nicely illustrated. New York, 1897.

VAN RENSSELAER, MRS. SCHUYLER, Art Out of Doors, New York, 1893. The most delightful book of all. Deals with the art, not with the practice, of gardening.

WEIDENMANN, J., Beautifying Country Homes, New York, 1870. A very handsome royal quarto volume, illustrated with numerous large colored plates showing the plans of places already improved.

INDEX.

	Page
Aconitum	125
Actinidia	142
Ageratum	132
Ailanthus	80
Akebia quinata	142
Alder	115
Alyssum	132
Amalanchier	115
American Gardening	145
Amherst, Alicia, book	146
Amorpha	115
Ampelopsis	142
André, Edouard, book	146
André, Edouard, quoted	40, 62, 87
Anemone	125
Annuals	129
Annual climbers	143
Antirrhinum	132
Appendix	145
Aquilegia	125
Aralia	115
Arbor day	97
Architectural features in gardening	36
Architectural style	26, 37
Architecture, rural	93
Aristolochia Sipho	142
Arnold Arboretum	16
Art and artist	3
Artificial constructions	21
Artistic qualities of landscape composition	9
Asclepias	125
Ash	108
Asters	125, 132
Atmosphere	68
Autumn colors	55
Bachelor's Button	133
Background	59
Backyard garden	5, 86, 130
Bacon, Lord Francis, essay	147
Bacon, Francis, quoted	53
Badly treated plants	25
Bailey, L. H., book	148
Bailey, L. H., quoted	10, 88
Balloon vine	143
Balsam	133
Balsam apple	144
Barberry	115
Basswood	110
Beech	108
Bienmueller, J., quoted	123
Bifurcations of drives and walks	74

	Page
Birch	108
Bluebell	126
Bocconia	126
Bois de Boulogne, Paris	22, 82
Boldness	31, 63
Books on landscape gardening	145
Borders	131
Border planting	124
Broken ground	45
Broken surface	41
Brooks	85
Bulbous plants	136
Burroughs, John	146
Butternut	108
Button bush	115
Calendula	133
Callirhoe	126
Calycanthus	115
Campanula	126
Candytuft	133
Caragana	115
Care of grounds	67
Cartolano, F., quoted	44, 62
Castor-oil bean	135
Catalpa	108
Cedar	108
Celastrus scandens	142
Celosia	133
Cemetery gardening	63
Centaurea	133
Central Park, New York	52
Cephalanthus	115
Cercis	116
Character	62
Cherries	119
Chionanthus	116
Choosing a style	29
Chrysanthemum	126
Cinquefoil	119
City lots	88
Cleanliness of grounds	67
Clematis	142
Clethra	116
Climbers	141
Climbing cucumber	143
Clipped trees	35
Cockscomb	133
Coffee tree	80, 109
Coherence	10
Color	36, 41, 51, 54, 55, 113
Columbine	125
Concourses	74
Coreopsis	126
Coreopsis, annual	133

	Page		Page
Cornus	116	Grouping	43, 57, 59
Cosmos	133	Guelder rose	122
Crocus	137	Hackberry	109
Curved lines	17, 48	Hardy perennials	96
Curves	73	Harebell	126
Cydonia	116	Hedges	24, 89
Dahlia	137	Helenium	126
Daphne	116	Helianthus	126
Datura	133	Hercules club	115
Deformed specimens	64	Hollyhock	126
Delphinium	126	Honey locust	109
Deutzia	116	Honeysuckle	119
Dianthus	133	Honeysuckle, climbing	143
Diervilla	116	Hop vine	143
Digitalis	126	Horse-chestnut	109
Dignity	63	Horticulturist	145
Distance	58	Hotel Ponce de Leon	11
Distance between trees	77	Howe, Walter, book	148
Dog's-tooth violet	137	Hunnewell, H. H., grounds	33
Dogwood	116	Hydrangea	118
Downing, A. J., books	148	Hypericum	118
Downing, A. J., quoted, 15, 76, 93, 97		Ipomoea	144
Drives	72	Iris	137
Dutchman's Pipe vine	142	Italian style	13, 26, 28, 33
Echinocystis lobata	143	Ivy	142
Elder	116, 117	Jaeger, H., books	147
Elaeagnus	117	"Jimpson Weed"	133
Elm	109	Judas tree	116
Elms for streets	35, 79	June	54
English style	13	Juneberry	115
Entrances	71	Karr, Alphonse, quoted	141
Erythronium	137	Kemp, Edward, quoted	66
Exochorda	117	Kerria	118
Exterior views	60	Koelreuteria	109
Farm house	94	Landscape architect	6
Farmyards	93	Landscape gardener	6
Fences	24, 96	Landscape gardening	3
Finish	66	Larkspur	126
Flagg, Wilson, quoted	113	Lawns	17, 32
Flat ground, treatment of	30	Lepachys	127
Flower beds	38, 131	Ligustrum	118
Foreground	47, 60	Lilac	119
Forsythia	117	Lily	138
Fountains	38	Linden	110
Foxglove	126	Lines, curved	17
Fringe tree	116	Long, E. A., book	148
Gaillardia	133	Long, E. A., quoted	141
Garden and Forest	145	Lonicera	119
Gardener	6	Lonicera, climbing	143
Gardener's materials	106	Loudon, J. C., book	147
Gardening	3	Loudon, Mrs., quoted	136
"Gay" style in gardening	87	Magnolias	110
General problems	70	Maples	110
Geometrical lines	31	Maple for streets	79
Geometrical style	26, 91	Mathews, F. Schuyler, quoted	44, 129
Geometrical style on flat ground	30	Maurandia	143
Gilpin, William, books	147	Maynard, Samuel T., book	148
Gilpin, William, quoted	40	Menispermum Canadense	143
Gilpin's idea of picturesqueness	41	Middle ground	60
Ginkgo trees	80, 109	Midsummer shade	55
Gladiolus	137	Military park entrance	73
Golden-Bell	117	Mina	143
Goldenrod	128	Mitchell, Donald G.	146
Grace	31	Momordica	144
Grouped trees	19	Monkshood	125
		Monstrosities	64

INDEX.

	Page
Monte Carlo	28
Moonseed	143
Morning Glory	144
Mountain scenery	41
Mulberry	110
Myrica	119
Narcissus	139
Nasturtium	134
Nasturtium, climbing	144
Naturalistic gardening	93
Naturalness, to gain	15
Naturalness, to lose	21
Natural style	15
Natural style in France	22
New England village streets	76
Oak	111
Œnothera	127
Oleaster	117
Olmsted, F. L., quoted	99
Olmsted, John C., quoted	81
Orpet, E. O., quoted	129
Palms for street planting	78
Pansy	134
Papaver	127
Park management	101
Park planting	99
Parks, uses of	99
Parsons, Samuel, Jr., books	148
Parsons, Samuel, Jr., quoted	81
Pattern bedding	38, 103
Paulownia	111
Pea tree	115
Pentstemon	128
Peony	128
Perennials	123
Perennial climbers	142
Petunia	134
Philadelphus	110
Phlox	128
Phlox Drummondii	134
Picturesque style	13, 40
Picturesque trees	40
Pine	111
Pinks	133
Ponds	83
Poplar	111
Poplars on streets	80
Poppy	127
Poppy, annual	135
Popular Gardening	145
Porches	141
Potentilla	119
Pot Marigold	131
Price, Sir Uvedale, essay	147
Privacy	89, 90
Privet	118
Propriety	63
Prospect Park, Brooklyn	47, 59, 102
Pruning	114
Prunus	119
Plane tree	112
Plans	12, 89
Platt, Charles A., book	148
Platt, Charles A., quoted	26
Plums	111, 119
Quince	116
Red bud	116

	Page
Repton, Humphrey, book	147
Rexford, E. E., quoted	136
Rhododendrons	120
Rhus	120
Ribes	120
Ricinus	135
Robinson, William, books	147
Robinson, William, quoted	113
Rockery	23
Rose, N. Jonsson, book	148
Roses	120
Rubus	121
Rudbeckia	128
Rural gardening	93
Rustic bridge	43
Rustic work	72
Sanitation, mental	100
Sargent, C. S., quoted	113
School grounds	97
Screen	59
Shad bush	115
Shade trees	94
Shenstone, William, book	147
Shrubs	18-20, 95, 98, 113
Simplicity	31, 62, 63
Single trees	58
Sky line	42, 49
Sloping ground	45
Snapdragon	132
Snowball	122
Snowberry	121
Solidago	128
Specifications	12
Spice bush	115
Spiræa	121, 128
Spring effects	54
Spruce	111
Stiles, W. A., quoted	99
Stocks	135
Straight lines	21
Street planting	34
Streets and avenues	76
Styles of gardening	40
Sub-tropical gardening	11
Suburban lots	88
Sumach	120
Summer houses	23
Sunflower	126
Sunflowers, annual	135
Surface	41, 45
Sweet gale	119
Sweet gum	112
Sweet pea	135, 144
Sycamore	112
Sycamore for streets	79
Symphoricarpus	121
Syringa	119
Table Mountain pine	42
Tecoma	143
Terraces	36
Texture	51-52
Thoreau	146
Thorn trees	112
Topiary work	35
Trailing vines	46
Transplanting annuals	131
Trees	107

	Page		Page
Trees analyzed	50	Vistas	49
Trees for shade	94	Walks	73
Tree rows	32	Walnut	112
Trellises	23	Warner, Charles Dudley	146
Trianon, Paris	84	Washington Park, Albany	49
Trillium	128	Water	46, 81
Tropæolum	134	Weather	68
Tropæolum, climbing	144	Weidenmann, J., book	148
Trumpet creeper	143	Weigelia	116
Tuberose	139	Wheatley, Thomas, book	147
Tulip	139	Wheatley, Thomas, quoted	40
Tulip tree	112	White surfaces	25
Union of building with grounds	20	Willows	112, 121
Unity	10, 89	Winter gardens	57
Van Dyke John C., quoted	10	Winter picture	56
Van Rensselaer, Mrs., book	148	Wistaria	143
Van Rensselaer, Mrs., quoted		World's Fair, Chicago	27
	3, 50, 51, 71	World's Fair grounds, Chicago,	
Variety	44		14, 37
Verbena	135	Yucca	140
Viburnum	122	Zinnias	125
Virgin's bower	142		

STANDARD BOOKS.

Forest Planting.

By H. NICHOLAS JARCHOW, LL. D. A treatise on the care of woodlands and the restoration of the denuded timberlands on plains and mountains. The author has fully described those European methods which have proved to be most useful in maintaining the superb forests of the old world. This experience has been adapted to the different climates and trees of America, full instructions being given for forest planting of our various kinds of soil and subsoil, whether on mountain or valley. Illustrated. 250 pages. 5x7 inches. Cloth. $1.50

Soils and Crops of the Farm.

By GEORGE E. MORROW, M. A., and THOMAS F. HUNT. The methods of making available the plant food in the soil are described in popular language. A short history of each of the farm crops is accompanied by a discussion of its culture. The useful discoveries of science are explained as applied in the most approved methods of culture. Illustrated. 310 pages. 5x7 inches. Cloth. $1.00

Land Draining.

A handbook for farmers on the principles and practice of draining, by MANLY MILES, giving the results of his extended experience in laying tile drains. The directions for the laying out and the construction of tile drains will enable the farmer to avoid the errors of imperfect construction, and the disappointment that must necessarily follow. This manual for practical farmers will also be found convenient for reference in regard to many questions that may arise in crop growing, aside from the special subjects of drainage of which it treats. Illustrated. 200 pages. 5x7 inches. Cloth. . . $1.00

Barn Plans and Outbuildings.

Two hundred and fifty-seven illustrations. A most valuable work, full of ideas, hints, suggestions, plans, etc., for the construction of barns and outbuildings, by practical writers. Chapters are devoted to the economic erection and use of barns, grain barns, horse barns, cattle barns, sheep barns, cornhouses, smokehouses, icehouses, pig pens, granaries, etc. There are likewise chapters on birdhouses, doghouses, tool sheds, ventilators, roofs and roofing, doors and fastenings, workshops, poultry houses, manure sheds, barnyards, root pits, etc. 235 pages. 5x7 inches. Cloth. . . . $1.00

STANDARD BOOKS.

Herbert's Hints to Horse Keepers.

By the late HENRY WILLIAM HERBERT (Frank Forester). This is one of the best and most popular works on the horse prepared in this country. A complete manual for horsemen, embracing: How to breed a horse; how to buy a horse; how to break a horse; how to use a horse; how to feed a horse; how to physic a horse (allopathy or homeopathy); how to groom a horse; how to drive a horse; how to ride a horse, etc. Beautifully illustrated. 425 pages. 5x7 inches. Cloth. $1.50

Diseases of Horses and Cattle.

By DR. D. MCINTOSH, V. S., professor of veterinary science in the university of Illinois. Written expressly for the farmer, stockman and veterinary student. A new work on the treatment of animal diseases, according to the modern status of veterinary science, has become a necessity. Such an one is this volume of over 400 pages, written by one of the most eminent veterinarians of our country. Illustrated. 426 pages. 5x7 inches. Cloth. $1.75

The Ice Crop.

By THERON L. HILES. How to harvest, ship and use ice. A complete, practical treatise for farmers, dairymen, ice dealers, produce shippers, meat packers, cold storers, and all interested in icehouses, cold storage, and the handling or use of ice in any way. Including many recipes for iced dishes and beverages. The book is illustrated by cuts of the tools and machinery used in cutting and storing ice, and the different forms of icehouses and cold storage buildings. Illustrated. 122 pages. 5x7 inches. Cloth. $1.00

The Secrets of Health, or How Not to Be Sick, and How to Get Well from Sickness.

By S. H. PLATT, A. M., M. D., late member of the Connecticut Eclectic Medical Society, the National Eclectic Medical Association, and honorary member of the National Bacteriological Society of America; our medical editor and author of "Talks With Our Doctor" and "Our Health Adviser." Nearly 600 pages. An index of 20 pages, so that any topic may be instantly consulted. A new departure in medical knowledge for the people—the latest progress, secrets and practices of all schools of healing made available for the common people—health without medicine, nature without humbug, common sense without folly, science without fraud. 81 illustrations. 576 pages. 5x7 inches. Cloth. $1.50

STANDARD BOOKS.

Hunter and Trapper.

By HALSEY THRASHER, an old and experienced sportsman. The best modes of hunting and trapping are fully explained, and foxes, deer, bears, etc., fall into his traps readily by following his directions. Illustrated. 92 pages. 5x7 inches. Cloth. $0.50

Batty's Practical Taxidermy and Home Decoration.

By JOSEPH H. BATTY, taxidermist for the government surveys and many colleges and museums in the United States. An entirely new and complete as well as authentic work on taxidermy—giving in detail full directions for collecting and mounting animals, birds, reptiles, fish, insects, and general objects of natural history. 125 illustrations. 204 pages. 5x7 inches. Cloth. $1.00

Hemp.

By S. S. BOYCE. A practical treatise on the culture of hemp for seed and fiber, with a sketch of the history and nature of the hemp plant. The various chapters are devoted to the soil and climate adapted to the culture of hemp for seed and for fiber, irrigating, harvesting, retting and machinery for handling hemp. Illustrated. 112 pages. 5x7 inches. Cloth. $0.50

Alfalfa.

By F. D. COBURN. Its growth, uses and feeding value. The fact that alfalfa thrives in almost any soil; that without reseeding, it goes on yielding two, three, four and sometimes five cuttings annually for five, ten, or perhaps 100 years; and that either green or cured it is one of the most nutritious forage plants known, makes reliable information upon its production and uses of unusual interest. Such information is given in this volume for every part of America, by the highest authority. Illustrated. 164 pages. 5x7 inches. Cloth. $0.50

Talks on Manure.

By JOSEPH HARRIS, M. S. A series of familiar and practical talks between the author and the deacon, the doctor, and other neighbors, on the whole subject of manures and fertilizers; including a chapter especially written for it by Sir John Bennet Lawes of Rothamsted, England. 366 pages. 5x7 inches. Cloth. $1.50

STANDARD BOOKS.

Practical Forestry.

By ANDREW S. FULLER. A treatise on the propagation, planting and cultivation, with descriptions and the botanical and popular names of all the indigenous trees of the United States, and notes on a large number of the most valuable exotic species. Illustrated. 300 pages. 5x7 inches. Cloth. $1.50

Irrigation for the Farm, Garden and Orchard.

By HENRY STEWART. This work is offered to those American farmers and other cultivators of the soil who, from painful experience, can readily appreciate the losses which result from the scarcity of water at critical periods. Fully illustrated. 276 pages. 5x7 inches. Cloth. . . $1.00

Irrigation Farming.

By LUTE WILCOX. A handbook for the practical application of water in the production of crops. A complete treatise on water supply, canal construction, reservoirs and ponds, pipes for irrigation purposes, flumes and their structure, methods of applying water, irrigation of field crops, the garden, the orchard and vineyard, windmills and pumps, appliances and contrivances. New edition, revised, enlarged and rewritten. Profusely illustrated. Over 500 pages. 5x7 inches. Cloth. $2.00

Ginseng, Its Cultivation, Harvesting, Marketing and Market Value.

By MAURICE G. KAINS, with a short account of its history and botany. It discusses in a practical way how to begin with either seed or roots, soil, climate and location, preparation, planting and maintenance of the beds, artificial propagation, manures, enemies, selection for market and for improvement, preparation for sale, and the profits that may be expected. This booklet is concisely written, well and profusely illustrated, and should be in the hands of all who expect to grow this drug to supply the export trade, and to add a new and profitable industry to their farms and gardens, without interfering with the regular work. New edition. Revised and enlarged. Illustrated. 5x7 inches. Cloth. . . . $0.50

Truck Farming at the South.

By A. OEMLER. A work giving the experience of a successful grower of vegetables or "garden truck" for northern markets. Essential to anyone who contemplates entering this profitable field of agriculture. Illustrated. 274 pages. 5x7 inches. Cloth. $1.00

STANDARD BOOKS.

Henderson's Practical Floriculture.

By PETER HENDERSON. A guide to the successful propagation and cultivation of florists' plants. The work is not one for florists and gardeners only, but the amateur's wants are constantly kept in mind, and we have a very complete treatise on the cultivation of flowers under glass, or in the open air, suited to those who grow flowers for pleasure as well as those who make them a matter of trade. New and enlarged edition. Beautifully illustrated. 325 pages. 5x7 inches. Cloth. $1.50

Mushrooms. How to Grow Them.

By WILLIAM FALCONER. This is the most practical work on the subject ever written, and the only book on growing mushrooms published in America. The author describes how he grows mushrooms, and how they are grown for profit by the leading market gardeners, and for home use by the most successful private growers. Engravings drawn from nature expressly for this work. 170 pages. 5x7 inches. Cloth. $1.00

Play and Profit in My Garden.

By E. P. ROE. The author takes us to his garden on the rocky hillsides in the vicinity of West Point, and shows us how out of it, after four years' experience, he evoked a profit of $1000, and this while carrying on pastoral and literary labor. It is very rarely that so much literary taste and skill are mated to so much agricultural experience and good sense. Illustrated. 350 pages. 5x7 inches. Cloth. . . $1.00

Fumigation Methods.

By WILLIS G. JOHNSON. A timely up-to-date book on the practical application of the new methods for destroying insects with hydrocyanic acid gas and carbon bisulphid, the most powerful insecticides ever discovered. It is an indispensable book for farmers, fruit growers, nurserymen, gardeners, florists, millers, grain dealers, transportation companies, college and experiment station workers, etc. Illustrated. 313 pages. 5x7 inches. Cloth. $1.00

Fungi and Fungicides.

By PROF. CLARENCE M. WEED. A practical manual concerning the fungous diseases of cultivated plants and the means of preventing their ravages. The author has endeavored to give such a concise account of the most important facts relating to these as will enable the cultivator to combat them intelligently. 90 illustrations. 222 pages. 5x7 inches. **Paper, 50 cents; cloth** $1.00

STANDARD BOOKS.

Insects and Insecticides.

By CLARENCE M. WEED, D. Sc., professor of entomology and zoology, New Hampshire college of agriculture. A practical manual concerning noxious insects, and methods of preventing their injuries. Many illustrations. 334 pages. 5x7 inches. Cloth. $1.50

How Crops Grow.

By PROF. SAMUEL W. JOHNSON of Yale college. New and revised edition. A treatise on the chemical composition, structure and life of the plant. This book is a guide to the knowledge of agricultural plants, their composition, their structure and modes of development and growth; of the complex organization of plants, and the use of the parts; the germination of seeds, and the food of plants obtained both from the air and the soil. The book is indispensable to all real students of agriculture. With numerous illustrations and tables of analysis. 416 pages. 5x7 inches. Cloth. $1.50

Tobacco Leaf.

By J. B. KILLEBREW and HERBERT MYRICK. Its Culture and Cure, Marketing and Manufacture. A practical handbook on the most approved methods in growing, harvesting, curing, packing and selling tobacco, with an account of the operations in every department of tobacco manufacture. The contents of this book are based on actual experiments in field, curing barn, packing house, factory and laboratory. It is the only work of the kind in existence, and is destined to be the standard practical and scientific authority on the whole subject of tobacco for many years. 506 pages and 150 original engravings. 5x7 inches. Cloth. $2.00

Coburn's Swine Husbandry.

By F. D. COBURN. New, revised and enlarged edition. The breeding, rearing and management of swine, and the prevention and treatment of their diseases. It is the fullest and freshest compendium relating to swine breeding yet offered. Illustrated. 312 pages. 5x7 inches. Cloth. $1.50

Home Pork Making.

The art of raising and curing pork on the farm. By A. W. FULTON. A complete guide for the farmer, the country butcher and the suburban dweller, in all that pertains to hog slaughtering, curing, preserving and storing pork product—from scalding vat to kitchen table and dining room. Illustrated. 125 pages. 5x7 inches. Cloth. . . . $0.50

STANDARD BOOKS.

Harris on the Pig.

By JOSEPH HARRIS. New edition. Revised and enlarged by the author. The points of the various English and American breeds are thoroughly discussed, and the great advantage of using thoroughbred males clearly shown. The work is equally valuable to the farmer who keeps but few pigs, and to the breeder on an extensive scale. Illustrated. 318 pages. 5x7 inches. Cloth. $1.00

The Dairyman's Manual.

By HENRY STEWART, author of "The Shepherd's Manual," "Irrigation," etc. A useful and practical work, by a writer who is well known as thoroughly familiar with the subject of which he writes. Illustrated. 475 pages. 5x7 inches. Cloth. $1.50

Feeds and Feeding.

By W. A. HENRY. This handbook for students and stockmen constitutes a compendium of practical and useful knowledge on plant growth and animal nutrition, feeding stuffs, feeding animals and every detail pertaining to this important subject. It is thorough, accurate and reliable, and is the most valuable contribution to live stock literature in many years. All the latest and best information is clearly and systematically presented, making the work indispensable to every owner of live stock. 658 pages. 6x9 inches. Cloth. . . $2.00

The Propagation of Plants.

By ANDREW S. FULLER. An eminently practical and useful work describing the process of hybridizing and crossing species and varieties and also the many different modes by which cultivated plants may be propagated and multiplied. Illustrated. 350 pages. 5x7 inches. Cloth. . . $1.50

Gardening for Pleasure.

By PETER HENDERSON. A guide to the amateur in the fruit, vegetable and flower garden, with full descriptions for the greenhouse, conservatory and window garden. It meets the wants of all classes in country, city and village, who keep a garden for their own enjoyment rather than for the sale of products. Finely illustrated. 404 pages. 5x7 inches. Cloth. $1.50

STANDARD BOOKS.

Prize Gardening.

Compiled by G. BURNAP FISKE. This unique book shows how to derive profit, pleasure and health from the garden, by giving the actual experiences of the successful prize winners in the American Agriculturist garden contest. Every line is from actual experience based on real work. The result is a mine and treasure house of garden practice, comprising the grand prize gardener's methods, gardening for profit, farm gardens, the home acre, town and city gardens, experimental gardening, methods under glass, success with specialties, prize flowers and fruits, gardening by women, boys and girls, irrigation, secrets, etc., etc. Illustrated from original photos. 320 pages. 5x7 inches. Cloth. $1.00

Gardening for Profit.

By PETER HENDERSON. The standard work on market and family gardening. The successful experience of the author for more than thirty years, and his willingness to tell, as he does in this work, the secret of his success for the benefit of others, enables him to give most valuable information. The book is profusely illustrated. 376 pages. 5x7 inches. Cloth. $1.50

The Window Flower Garden.

By JULIUS J. HEINRICH. The author is a practical florist, and this enterprising volume embodies his personal experience in window gardening during a long period. New and enlarged edition. Illustrated. 123 pages. 5x7 inches. Cloth. $0.50

Market Gardening and Farm Notes.

By BURNETT LANDRETH. Experiences and observation for both north and south, of interest to the amateur gardener, trucker and farmer. A novel feature of the book is the calendar of farm and garden operations for each month of the year; the chapters on fertilizers, transplanting, succession and rotation of crops, the packing, shipping and marketing of vegetables will be especially useful to market gardeners. 315 pages. 5x7 inches. Cloth. $1.00

The Study of Breeds.

By THOMAS SHAW. Origin, history, distribution, characteristics, adaptability, uses, and standards of excellence of all pedigreed breeds of cattle, sheep and swine in America. The accepted text book in colleges, and the authority for farmers and breeders. Illustrated. 371 pages. 5x7 inches. Cloth. $1.50

STANDARD BOOKS.

Animal Breeding.

By THOMAS SHAW. This book is the most complete and comprehensive work ever published on the subject of which it treats. It is the first book which has systematized the subject of animal breeding. The leading laws which govern this most intricate question the author has boldly defined and authoritatively arranged. The chapters which he has written on the more involved features of the subject, as sex and the relative influence of parents, should go far toward setting at rest the wildly speculative views cherished with reference to these questions. The striking originality in the treatment of the subject is no less conspicuous than the superb order and regular sequence of thought from the beginning to the end of the book. The book is intended to meet the needs of all persons interested in the breeding and rearing of live stock. Illustrated. 405 pages. 5x7 inches. Cloth. . . $1.50

Forage Crops Other Than Grasses.

By THOMAS SHAW. How to cultivate, harvest and use them. Indian corn, sorghum, clover, leguminous plants, crops of the brassica genus, the cereals, millet, field roots, etc. Intensely practical and reliable. Illustrated. 287 pages. 5x7 inches. Cloth. $1.00

Soiling Crops and the Silo.

By THOMAS SHAW. The growing and feeding of all kinds of soiling crops, conditions to which they are adapted, their plan in the rotation, etc. Not a line is repeated from the Forage Crops book. Best methods of building the silo, filling it and feeding ensilage. Illustrated. 364 pages. 5x7 inches. Cloth. $1.50

Stewart's Shepherd's Manual.

By HENRY STEWART. A valuable practical treatise on the sheep for American farmers and sheep growers. It is so plain that a farmer or a farmer's son who has never kept a sheep may learn from its pages how to manage a flock successfully, and yet so complete that even the experienced shepherd may gather many suggestions from it. The results of personal experience of some years, with the characters of the various modern breeds of sheep, and the sheep raising capabilities of many portions of our extensive territory and that of Canada—and the careful study of the diseases to which our sheep are chiefly subject, with those by which they may eventually be afflicted through unforeseen accidents—as well as the methods of management called for under our circumstances, are carefully described. Illustrated. 276 pages. 5x7 inches. Cloth. $1.00

STANDARD BOOKS.

Pear Culture for Profit.

By P. T. Quinn, practical horticulturist. Teaching how to raise pears intelligently, and with the best results, how to find out the character of the soil, the best methods of preparing it, the best varieties to select under existing conditions, the best modes of planting, pruning, fertilizing, grafting, and utilizing the ground before the trees come into bearing, and, finally, of gathering and packing for market. Illustrated. 136 pages. 5x7 inches. Cloth. $1.00

Cranberry Culture.

By Joseph J. White. Contents: Natural history, history of cultivation, choice of location, preparing the ground, planting the vines, management of meadows, flooding, enemies and difficulties overcome, picking, keeping, profit and loss. Illustrated. 132 pages. 5x7 inches. Cloth. . . $1.00

Ornamental Gardening for Americans.

By Elias A. Long, landscape architect. A treatise on beautifying homes, rural districts and cemeteries. A plain and practical work with numerous illustrations and instructions so plain that they may be readily followed. Illustrated. 390 pages. 5x7 inches. Cloth. $1.50

Grape Culturist.

By A. S. Fuller. This is one of the very best of works on the culture of the hardy grapes, with full directions for all departments of propagation, culture, etc., with 150 excellent engravings, illustrating planting, training, grafting, etc. 282 pages. 5x7 inches. Cloth. $1.50

Gardening for Young and Old.

By Joseph Harris. A work intended to interest farmers' boys in farm gardening, which means a better and more profitable form of agriculture. The teachings are given in the familiar manner so well known in the author's "Walks and Talks on the Farm." Illustrated. 191 pages. 5x7 inches. Cloth. $1.00

Money in the Garden.

By P. T. Quinn. The author gives in a plain, practical style instructions on three distinct although closely connected branches of gardening—the kitchen garden, market garden and field culture, from successful practical experience for a term of years. Illustrated. 268 pages. 5x7 inches. Cloth. $1.00

STANDARD BOOKS.

Plums and Plum Culture.

By F. A. WAUGH. A complete manual for fruit growers, nurserymen, farmers and gardeners, on all known varieties of plums and their successful management. This book marks an epoch in the horticultural literature of America. It is a complete monograph of the plums cultivated in and indigenous to North America. It will be found indispensable to the scientist seeking the most recent and authoritative information concerning this group, to the nurseryman who wishes to handle his varieties accurately and intelligently, and to the cultivator who would like to grow plums successfully. Illustrated. 391 pages. 5x7 inches. Cloth. . . . $1.50

Fruit, Harvesting, Storing, Marketing.

By F. A. WAUGH. A practical guide to the picking, storing, shipping and marketing of fruit. The principal subjects covered are the fruit market, fruit picking, sorting and packing, the fruit storage, evaporating, canning, statistics of the fruit trade, fruit package laws, commission dealers and dealing, cold storage, etc., etc. No progressive fruit grower can afford to be without this most valuable book. Illustrated. 232 pages. 5x7 inches. Cloth. $1.00

The Fruit Garden.

By P. BARRY. A standard work on fruit and fruit trees, the author having had over thirty years' practical experience at the head of one of the largest nurseries in this country. Invaluable to all fruit growers. Illustrated. 516 pages. 5x7 inches. Cloth. $1.50

The Nut Culturist.

By ANDREW S. FULLER. A treatise on the propagation, planting and cultivation of nut-bearing trees and shrubs adapted to the climate of the United States, with the scientific and common names of the fruits known in commerce as edible or otherwise useful nuts. Intended to aid the farmer to increase his income without adding to his expenses or labor. Illustrated. 290 pages. 5x7 inches. Cloth. . . $1.50

American Grape Growing and Wine Making.

By GEORGE HUSMANN of California. New and enlarged edition. With contributions from well-known grape growers, giving wide range of experience. The author of this book is a recognized authority on the subject. Illustrated. 269 pages. 5x7 inches. Cloth. $1.50

STANDARD BOOKS.

Turkeys and How to Grow Them.

Edited by HERBERT MYRICK. A treatise on the natural history and origin of the name of turkeys; the various breeds, the best methods to insure success in the business of turkey growing. With essays from practical turkey growers in different parts of the United States and Canada. Copiously illustrated. 154 pages. 5x7 inches. Cloth. . . $1.00

Profits in Poultry.

Useful and ornamental breeds and their profitable management. This excellent work contains the combined experience of a number of practical men in all departments of poultry raising. It forms a unique and important addition to our poultry literature. Profusely illustrated. 352 pages. 5x7 inches. Cloth. $1.00

The New Egg Farm.

By H. H. STODDARD. A practical, reliable manual upon producing eggs and poultry for market as a profitable business enterprise, either by itself or connected with other branches of agriculture. It tells all about how to feed and manage, how to breed and select, incubators and brooders, its labor-saving devices, etc., etc. Illustrated. 331 pages. 5x7 inches. Cloth. $1.00

Treat's Injurious Insects of the Farm and Garden.

By MRS. MARY TREAT. An original investigator who has added much to our knowledge of both plants and insects, and those who are familiar with Darwin's works are aware that he gives her credit for important observation and discoveries. New and enlarged edition. With an illustrated chapter on beneficial insects. Fully illustrated. 296 pages. 5x7 inches. Cloth. $1.50

The Dogs of Great Britain, America and Other Countries.

New, enlarged and revised edition. Their breeding, training and management, in health and disease; comprising all the essential parts of the two standard works on dogs by "Stonehenge." It describes the best game and hunting grounds in America. Contains over one hundred beautiful engravings, embracing most noted dogs in both continents, making, together with chapters by American writers, the most complete dog book ever published. 370 pages. 5x7 inches. Cloth. $1.50

STANDARD BOOKS.

Landscape Gardening.

By F. A. WAUGH, professor of horticulture, university of Vermont. A treatise on the general principles governing outdoor art; with sundry suggestions for their application in the commoner problems of gardening. Every paragraph is short, terse and to the point, giving perfect clearness to the discussions at all points. In spite of the natural difficulty of presenting abstract principles the whole matter is made entirely plain even to the inexperienced reader. Illustrated. 152 pages. 5x7 inches. Cloth. $0.50

Hedges, Windbreaks, Shelters and Live Fences.

By E. P. POWELL. A treatise on the planting, growth and management of hedge plants for country and suburban homes. It gives accurate directions concerning hedges; how to plant and how to treat them; and especially concerning windbreaks and shelters. It includes the whole art of making a delightful home, giving directions for nooks and balconies, for bird culture and for human comfort. Illustrated. 140 pages. 5x7 inches. Cloth. $0.50

The New Rhubarb Culture.

A complete guide to dark forcing and field culture. Part I—By J. E. MORSE, the well-known Michigan trucker and originator of the now famous and extremely profitable new methods of dark forcing and field culture. Part II—Compiled by G. B. FISKE. Other methods practiced by the most experienced market gardeners, greenhouse men and experimenters in all parts of America. Illustrated. 130 pages. 5x7 inches. Cloth. $0.50

Greenhouse Construction.

By PROF. L. R. TAFT. A complete treatise on greenhouse structures and arrangements of the various forms and styles of plant houses for professional florists as well as amateurs. All the best and most approved structures are so fully and clearly described that anyone who desires to build a greenhouse will have no difficulty in determining the kind best suited to his purpose. The modern and most successful methods of heating and ventilating are fully treated upon. Special chapters are devoted to houses used for the growing of one kind of plants exclusively. The construction of hotbeds and frames receives appropriate attention. Over one hundred excellent illustrations, specially engraved for this work, make every point clear to the reader and add considerably to the artistic appearance of the book. 210 pages. 5x7 inches. Cloth. $1.50

STANDARD BOOKS.

Greenhouse Management.

By L. R. Taft. This book forms an almost indispensable companion volume to Greenhouse Construction. In it the author gives the results of his many years' experience, together with that of the most successful florists and gardeners, in the management of growing plants under glass. So minute and practical are the various systems and methods of growing and forcing roses, violets, carnations, and all the most important florists' plants, as well as fruits and vegetables described, that by a careful study of this work and the following of its teachings, failure is almost impossible. Illustrated. 382 pages. 5x7 inches. Cloth. $1.50

Bulbs and Tuberous-Rooted Plants.

By C. L. Allen. A complete treatise on the history, description, methods of propagation and full directions for the successful culture of bulbs in the garden, dwelling and greenhouse. The author of this book has for many years made bulb growing a specialty, and is a recognized authority on their cultivation and management. The cultural directions are plainly stated, practical and to the point. The illustrations which embellish this work have been drawn from nature and have been engraved especially for this book. 312 pages. 5x7 inches. Cloth. . . . $1.50

Cabbage, Cauliflower and Allied Vegetables.

By C. L. Allen. A practical treatise on the various types and varieties of cabbage, cauliflower, broccoli, Brussels sprouts, kale, collards and kohl-rabi. An explanation is given of the requirements, conditions, cultivation and general management pertaining to the entire cabbage group. After this each class is treated separately and in detail. The chapter on seed raising is probably the most authoritative treatise on this subject ever published. Insects and fungi attacking this class of vegetables are given due attention. Illustrated. 126 pages. 5x7 inches. Cloth. $0.50

Asparagus.

By F. M. Hexamer. This is the first book published in America which is exclusively devoted to the raising of asparagus for home use as well as for market. It is a practical and reliable treatise on the saving of the seed, raising of the plants, selection and preparation of the soil, planting, cultivation, manuring, cutting, bunching, packing, marketing, canning and drying, insect enemies, fungous diseases and every requirement to successful asparagus culture, special emphasis being given to the importance of asparagus as a farm and money crop. Illustrated. 174 pages. 5x7 inches. Cloth. $0.50

www.ingramcontent.com/pod-product-compliance
Lightning Source LLC
Chambersburg PA
CBHW020259170426
43202CB00008B/434